# WHERE EQUITY LIVES

# Where Equity Lives
*Eliminating Systemic Inequity Traps in Schools and Districts*

## Robin Avelar La Salle and Ruth S. Johnson

Foreword by Michael Fullan

ROWMAN & LITTLEFIELD
*Lanham • Boulder • New York • London*

Published by Rowman & Littlefield
An imprint of The Rowman & Littlefield Publishing Group, Inc.
4501 Forbes Boulevard, Suite 200, Lanham, Maryland 20706
www.rowman.com

86-90 Paul Street, London EC2A 4NE

Copyright © 2023 by Robin Avelar La Salle and Ruth S. Johnson

Book Cover Artist: Tati La Salle

*All rights reserved.* No part of this book may be reproduced in any form or by any electronic or mechanical means, including information storage and retrieval systems, without written permission from the publisher, except by a reviewer who may quote passages in a review.

British Library Cataloguing in Publication Information Available

**Library of Congress Cataloging-in-Publication Data**

Names: La Salle, Robin Avelar, author. | Johnson, Ruth S., author.
Title: Where equity lives : eliminating systemic inequity traps in schools and districts / Robin Avelar La Salle and Ruth S. Johnson.
Description: Lanham, Maryland : Rowman & Littlefield, 2023. | Includes bibliographical references and index. | Summary: "This book is the result of 25 years of studying over 300 schools and districts struggling to overturn the long-standing pattern of under achievement of the same demographic groups. It is a reveal of the five most common systemic inequity traps identified through the Study of Studies and ways for leaders to ameliorate them"—Provided by publisher.
Identifiers: LCCN 2023010822 (print) | LCCN 2023010823 (ebook) | ISBN 9781475866902 (cloth) | ISBN 9781475866919 (paperback) | ISBN 9781475866926 (epub)
Subjects: LCSH: Educational equalization—United States. | Academic achievement—United States. | School improvement programs—United States.
Classification: LCC LC213.2 .L386 2023  (print) | LCC LC213.2  (ebook) | DDC 379.2/60973—dc23/eng/20230403
LC record available at https://lccn.loc.gov/2023010822
LC ebook record available at https://lccn.loc.gov/2023010823

*To all who believe that every student is entitled to a premium education,
no matter where they go to school.*

## Contents

Preface: A Tale of Two Boys . . . . . . . . . . . . . . . . . . . . . . ix
Acknowledgments . . . . . . . . . . . . . . . . . . . . . . . . . . . xv
Foreword . . . . . . . . . . . . . . . . . . . . . . . . . . . . . . . xvii

Introduction . . . . . . . . . . . . . . . . . . . . . . . . . . . . . . . 1

**Part I: What's the Floor?**
CHAPTER 1: Symbolic Data Systems
Equity Hook: The Emperor's New Clothes . . . . . . . . . . . . . 9

CHAPTER 2: Baby-Steps Planning
Equity Hook: Backcast, Don't Forecast . . . . . . . . . . . . . . .33

**Part II: Under What Conditions?**
CHAPTER 3: New Tracking
Equity Hook: A Rose by Any Other Name . . . . . . . . . . . . .51

CHAPTER 4: The Christmas Tree Effect
Equity Hook: The Thing of the Thing . . . . . . . . . . . . . . . .77

**Part III: How Aligned Are YOU?**
CHAPTER 5: Misaligned Leadership
Equity Hook: Equity Leadership Columns . . . . . . . . . . . . .97

Conclusion . . . . . . . . . . . . . . . . . . . . . . . . . . . . . . 115
Appendix A . . . . . . . . . . . . . . . . . . . . . . . . . . . . . . 119
References . . . . . . . . . . . . . . . . . . . . . . . . . . . . . . . 123
Index . . . . . . . . . . . . . . . . . . . . . . . . . . . . . . . . . . 127
About the Authors . . . . . . . . . . . . . . . . . . . . . . . . . . 133

# Preface

## *A Tale of Two Boys*

Sal Castro High School held a student study team (SST) meeting where a teacher, counselor, school psychologist, special education case manager, and administrator met monthly on a Friday to discuss individual students in need of support. On one Friday two tenth graders, Luke and Lucio, were on the agenda for virtually the same set of concerns, which included the following:

- B-average grades, but slipping
- C or D grades on recent in-class exams
- history of scoring "just below grade level" on state academic proficiency exams
- regularly missed homework assignments
- satisfactory attendance but frequent tardies
- asking to leave during class or before class is over to visit the restroom at times
- distracted, quiet, and not disrespectful but not very engaged

The students and their parents were invited to the SST meeting.

### Student No. 1: Luke

The SST staff members sat on one side of a conference table. Right on time, the entrance door opened and in came Luke's parents. They stepped into the meeting room with a serious energy. Following them were two people who introduced themselves as a private school psychologist and a parent advocate. After their entrance came an attorney. Luke was the last to enter the room, lighthearted and relaxed. They all sat across from the school personnel.

The principal opened the meeting by saying, "Thank you all for attending today. The purpose of the SST convening is to discuss Luke's academic performance and to brainstorm—" Just then, the attorney interrupted and placed a thick report on the table in front of the principal. He explained that Luke's private advocacy team reviewed his case and wrote a report with the following summary, written in these exact words:

- Luke is college bound, so all decisions must support that end.
- Luke was diagnosed with School Aversion Disorder, a disability that explains his tardiness, early exits from class, and missed homework assignments.
- For Luke to graduate high school with college eligibility, he requires the following special considerations:
  - Luke must receive no penalties for tardiness or leaving class at any time.
  - Luke needs several makeup opportunities for missed assignments. However, he must receive no penalties for missed assignments.
  - Any time Luke gets less than an A on an in-class exam, he requires a makeup opportunity to retake the exam at home, proctored by a parent.

Also, given his college trajectory, Luke is to remain in the most prestigious and rigorous program offered at Sal Castro High. For him to receive maximum benefit from his classes, Luke requires the following supports:
- Teachers in every class should frequently check that he is keeping up and should provide small group support during class whenever he starts to get off track.

- Luke should be seated in the front row of every class so teachers can easily help him individually when he needs it so he can keep up with the rest of the class.
- He needs a separate designated time during the day where someone can review major points from his daily lessons. Here he can get a preview of lessons for the following day so he can better keep up the following day. He should also get support with organization and keeping up with assignments.
- If Luke struggles with any concepts by the end of the day, he should have access to a tutor. He should have the same tutor all the time.

The meeting ended in twenty tense minutes. Taking cues from the principal, the school team said very little. The list of considerations was documented and accepted. Everyone signed off on them. Then Luke's team stood up in unison and walked out of the door on the opposite side of the room from where they entered.

## Student No. 2: Lucio

No sooner had Luke's team exited through one door when the entrance door opened. Lucio nervously walked in beside his mother, who also appeared uncomfortable. They sat across from the school team of five educators. The principal asked about Lucio's father. Lucio explained that his father could not leave work or his employer would dock his pay. His mother worked the very early shift, so she was able to come to this midday meeting right from work.

The principal thanked Lucio's mother for attending and explained that the purpose of the SST was to discuss Lucio's academic performance and to brainstorm ways to help him improve. At that point Lucio raised his hand to say that his mother understood some English but was not fluent. None of the school team members were bilingual, so the principal asked Lucio if he would translate for his mother. Lucio agreed. Each of the school team members gave their report about Lucio, and he

## Preface

translated for his mother in the way *he understood* the information. The following is an excerpt from that exchange.

Teacher: Lucio is having difficulties with his academics, and we are here to seek ways to address them.

[English translation of what Lucio said to his mother in Spanish]: They say that I'm a bad student and they don't know what do.

School psychologist: It is important for Lucio to be on time to school every day, and to stay for the entire class. When he misses class time, he is not able to complete his assignments because he misses important information. Then he does not do well on his exams.

[Lucio's translation (with head bowed, eyes pointed down toward his mom's feet)]: They say that I'm not good. They say that I don't do what I'm supposed to do, so I am failing. I am a failure.

Special education teacher: Do you know if you have any diagnosed learning disabilities identified by your previous district?

[Lucio's translation (after a long blink)]: They say something is wrong with me. They want to know what is wrong with me. I don't know.

Principal: Do you have any questions? We want to make things easier for Lucio so he can graduate.

[Lucio's translation to his mother (his and his mother's eyes are welled up)]: They asked if you want to say anything.

Lucio [answering for her]: No, my mom has no words.

Even though they did not understand what Lucio said to his mother, the team felt the soul-crushing heaviness that Lucio and his mother tried to hide during the one-hour meeting. The team shared an unspoken inference that the family must be experiencing unusually difficult stressors for Lucio and his mom to respond so emotionally to this routine meeting.

So with great empathy, the principal offered the following suggestion to the SST team of educators. "Why don't we move Lucio to the alternative high school? That school does not require the college-eligibility courses provided at Sal Castro High. They offer simpler versions of core classes, like life science instead of biology and 'math for life' rather than algebra. The school is great at helping students get credits and graduate."

    Principal: How would you like that, Lucio? You are probably coming late and leaving during class because the work is too hard for you, or you are having other problems at home. You are a fine young man, and moving to the continuation school will make life easier for you. How does that sound to your mom?

    [Lucio's translation (almost in a whisper, his voice cracking)]: They are kicking me out of my school. They are sending me to the school for bad kids. [He pauses a moment.] I'm sorry, mother. Forgive me.

    The meeting ended. Lucio extended his hand to help his mother up from her seat. She attempted a smile at the school team and said, "Thank you." Lucio and his mom left out of the same door that Luke's team exited the previous hour.

    The following Monday, Luke returned to school with no changes to his schedule of classes. By then the principal had already explained to every teacher the legal obligations they needed to meet to comply with the written agreement from Luke's private advocacy team. Simultaneously, Lucio reported to the alternative school office for what they called intake.

    After the SST meeting, neither boy's profile changed much, except that Luke's grades improved and Lucio's declined. Two years later, Luke graduated with plenty of fanfare from the stands. Then he went on to a university that agreed to the same special considerations he had in high school. This is because once educational considerations are documented in one school, it is common practice to have them extend to other schools or colllleges.

    As for Lucio, the counselor who was on his SST team attended the alternative high school graduation and asked the principal, "What ever happened to Lucio? He was not at the graduation." The principal responded, "I have not thought about Lucio in years. I really don't know." When the principal went back to his office, he looked for Lucio's name in the district registry. His name no longer appeared on the roster at any district school and no other district ever requested his records. The counselor flashed back to the SST meeting two years prior. She was flooded by the overwhelming weight she felt observing Lucio and his mother during the meeting. She paused for a melancholy moment in the middle of the graduation hoopla and thought to herself, "And Lucio's mom thanked us. Wow."

- How do you feel reading this true story?
- Why do things like this still occur in this day and age?
- Has anything like this ever happened in your school system?
- Does your sense of basic fairness make you feel like you must do something to help all the Lucios and Lucias in our school systems?
- Are you asking yourself what you can do to make sure this never happens again to another student and family?

If so, we invite you to join the community of education leaders who feel as you do and read on.

# Acknowledgments

We thank everyone involved in the preparation of this book. Martha Avelar, your help analyzing the three hundred–plus cases in our study of studies was invaluable. We appreciate you as a colleague, and I (Robin) adore you as my sister. Thank you, Tati La Salle, for the inspiring book cover design. Also, thank you, Coco La Salle and Darian Conard, for making it possible to have Darian's memorable picture on the cover.

Everyone from our Orenda Education family, you were so supportive for almost a year as we worked on this book. With your daily work in schools and districts, you demonstrate that "$X$ marks the spot" is possible. For your contributions to the book, we thank Cynthia Herrera and Carlye Marousek for chapter 1; Sarah Gonzales for chapter 3; Janet Hwang and Genny Sosa for chapter 4; and Scott McGuire, Jeanette Salinas, and Christine Rich for chapter 5. Thank you, Marty Maya, for your wisdom and experience that are threaded throughout the pages of this book. Sara Shankin, we are indebted to you for your heavy systemic data analyses in almost all the case studies represented in the book.

We would not have been able complete this research and write this book without the support of Randy Barth, CEO of Think Together, Orenda's parent organization. We are eternally grateful to you and the entire board of trustees. In particular, Sang Peruri and Dan Young, thank you for championing our work from the inception of the Orenda–Think Together relationship.

We appreciate the love and support from our families. Led by David (Robin's business partner, husband, and the captain of our booster club), our families have cheered us on despite the sacrifices they've made so we can do what we feel we must. You mean everything to us.

## Acknowledgments

Finally, this is a note to Ruth Johnson from me, Robin. Ruth, you have been my colleague, mentor, friend, and family for a long, long time. I am the luckiest person I know because, for some reason, you chose to share your experience, expertise, and wisdom with me. In everything you say and do, you set the standard for what I want to become as an educator and as a genuinely good human being. Thank you for investing over twenty years into my personal and professional growth. Thank you for sharing decades of your life with me. I respect you, and I love you more than you'll ever know.

# Foreword

What's up with *equity*? It has received nonstop attention from states and the federal government in the United States since the 1970s. With greater and greater investments, there is more and more inequity. La Salle and Johnson's careful study of actual examples of greater equity allows us to dissect and understand the levers of greater equity and to get inside the problem with the goal of finally turning around this pernicious and relentless trend. I'll give you my conclusion first and then unpack it.

Reversing the trend won't be easy because the problem and solution are nuanced. Fortunately, La Salle and Johnson are "nuancers" and give us what we need to delve into the problem and the possible solution (or, more accurately, the lines of the solutions). The reason that they can do this is that they have spent twenty-five years studying and working in the problem. And they have kept track of what they have learned. Thus, their database has over three hundred studies; they call it the study of studies. They claim that the results "provide equity leaders a way to get past good intentions and move to shatter long-standing systemic inequities in education, once and for all."

But wait a minute. The problem is complex, and the solutions are nuanced. Don't expect to be served the solution on a platter. Readers will have to do their part in interpreting the findings and, equally, in figuring out how to address their own settings. My foreword is intended to focus on this personal matter: How can this book help me in my situation? For starters, the authors reveal "the five most common, most ubiquitous, and most injurious systemic inequity traps." Here is a nuance for you: knowing a trap does not tell you how to avoid it or get out of it, and knowing how to get out of the trap does not tell you how to find salvation. I am saying all this to stress that the reader and their group are going to have to do a lot of careful, insightful work to reverse the talons of inequity that have been with us in the two hundred years since the founding of public schools.

Now, let us move to the five chapters that tell us about the five traps. Remember, from the moment you think about the traps, start formulating your pathway out of them, starting with the question of why each trap has existed so long and is so well ensconced. The five traps are symbolic data systems (that absent clarity about academic expectation for every child); how to get at underlying organizational beliefs and expectations for all students to excel academically; how tracking creeps into education systems with devastating consequences; the Christmas tree effect (what the authors call *program shopping*); and misaligned leadership (how alignment of leaders at the front end is a nonstarter).

There. Hopefully, I have set the reader up with enough intrigue that they can enter the book as a proactive consumer. Let me offer my own system-change-oriented interpretation that also bends the reader toward a solution to the so-far-fruitless attempts to reverse the needle of inequity. I think there are two big reasons why we have made reverse progress when it comes to inequity—both figure in the plot. One is that society is prejudiced against certain individuals and groups (know that you don't have to be conscious of your bias to be discriminatory). In the wider work, including La Salle and Johnson's, as well as ours, the goal is that for both social justice and for what's-good-for-all reasons, present and future societies would be better off (and, indeed, our very survival may depend on it) if we could become equitable.

The other reason may be more practical about what one should do about *the change process*. Strictly from a change process perspective, the five traps wreak with bad strategy: vague pathways, too many variables at once, absence of coherence, wrong or immeasurable outcomes, poor leadership, and so on. Here is my final piece of advice: as you go from bad trap to best trail in this book, extract an approach to change in your own situation that contains no more than four or five priorities, or key factors; this involves those who are expected to benefit the change in helping to determine it (what we call *joint determination*) and in considering what constitutes progress and, above all, learning how to achieve "specificity without imposition."

In short, use this great book with its deep and plentiful ideas to help you figure out and better advance your own change situation. Use the book to help you answer the ironic question: Why is it that the more we focus on equity, the worse it becomes? Perhaps the first answer, as Avelar La Salle and Johnson basically say, is that "we have not yet seriously focused on equity." As the book promises, "find out where equity lives!"

    Michael Fullan, professor emeritus OISE/University of Toronto

# Introduction

Let's jump right in. Be bold. Be honest. Be vulnerable. Answer these three questions:

- Are you aware that the United States has persistent achievement gaps between demographic groups, and these patterns have existed for over two centuries?
- Do you lament that our educational system appears to advantage some students and disadvantage others?
- Are you generally familiar with the characteristics of successful schools?

Many, if not most, educators likely answered yes to at least two questions.

Let us continue our bold and honest odyssey. Table I.1 presents a version of what has become an almost iconic short list of well-known commonalities of the most impactful schools for historically lower-achieving students.

Reflect on each question, and respond yes or no to each question in table I.1.

Table I.1 has a possible maximum of twelve yes answers. Most of you likely responded with at least eight affirmative responses. So, as advocates of educational fairness, here is our quandary: *If* we

- know that historic gaps exist;

## Introduction

- recognize that school systems have practices that advantage some student groups and disadvantage others;
- are aware that high-performing schools for historically low-achieving districts share a set of best practices; and
- serve in schools, districts, and institutions working in earnest to provide a premium education to every student,

**Table I.1** Characteristics of Impactful Schools

| *Directions: Mark an X representing yes or no for each question related to each characteristic.* | Is this characteristic familiar to you? | | Is your school, district, or institution working on implementing this element? | |
|---|---|---|---|---|
| | Yes | No | Yes | No |
| 1. Effective district and school leadership | | | | |
| 2. Clear and focused system to improve teaching and learning for all students | | | | |
| 3. Safe and student-centered environment | | | | |
| 4. Culture of high expectations for students and adults, regardless of demographics | | | | |
| 5. Clear goals and frequent monitoring of student progress | | | | |
| 6. Access to a premium-level education for all students with built-in necessary supports | | | | |
| Total your yes responses for each column: | | | | |

NOTE: THESE CHARACTERISTICS ARE OFTEN ASSOCIATED WITH RESEARCHERS SUCH AS BLANKSTEIN, NOGUERA, AND KELLY (2016); BARTH (1999); LEZOTTE (1991); AND EDMONDS (2020).

INTRODUCTION

then why is the achievement of historically lower-achieving students still lagging? Why haven't those student outcome gaps (including nonacademic ones, such as discipline) closed?

Since the publication of our book *Shattering Inequities: Real-World Wisdom for School and District Leaders* (Avelar La Salle and Johnson 2018), readers and presentation audiences have asked us for specific guidance on persistent and enigmatic educational questions. We have answered the call! This new book helps leaders

- understand and identify the most common inequity traps that create anchors on the educational attainment of some student groups (most often, African American, Latino, Native American, and lower income students) and
- release those traps and replace them with irrefutably effective practices that accelerate academic success for historically lower-achieving students.

How will we do that? This guidance is a reveal of leadership truths gleaned from an exhaustive review of over three hundred studies and twenty thousand pages of analyses, having been conducted over a quarter of a century.

Over the past twenty-five years, we, together with the highly knowledgeable and skilled educational specialists at Orenda Education (1997–2022), studied schools and districts struggling to break the cycle of historical and persistently poor student academic outcomes for students of color and poor students. The three hundred studies that resulted in this book represent urban, rural, small, large, elementary, secondary, unified, comprehensive, alternative, juvenile detention, and tribal schools and districts.

Based on this "study of studies," we reveal the five most *common*, most *ubiquitous*, and most *injurious* systemic inequity traps. These practices have plagued school systems for longer than our studies document and continue to exist today only in more "modern" ways, as we will demonstrate.

INTRODUCTION

This book provides equity leaders with rich, timely, and unambiguous guidance to get past good intentions and move to shatter long-standing systemic inequities in education once and for all. It is a tall order, but we know that it is possible and that it need not take any more lost generations of students. Figure I.1 depicts the five most common systemic inequity traps organized by three questions we think should take center stage at any gathering of adults who care about educational justice.

Every chapter has two titles. The first is a traditional title, and the second is an "equity hook" based on linguistic and visual metaphors. Equity hooks serve as emotional and cognitive triggers to allow readers to automatically retrieve the spirit and the emotion, as well as the insights, associated with each chapter. Chapter 1, for example, is entitled "Symbolic Data Systems." It is accompanied by the mysterious equity hook, "The Emperor's New Clothes," the meaning of which will become clear as you read the chapter!

Each chapter contains major concepts and principles from research sandwiched between true stories of equity champions who tangled with the most common systemic missed opportunities. Stories describe

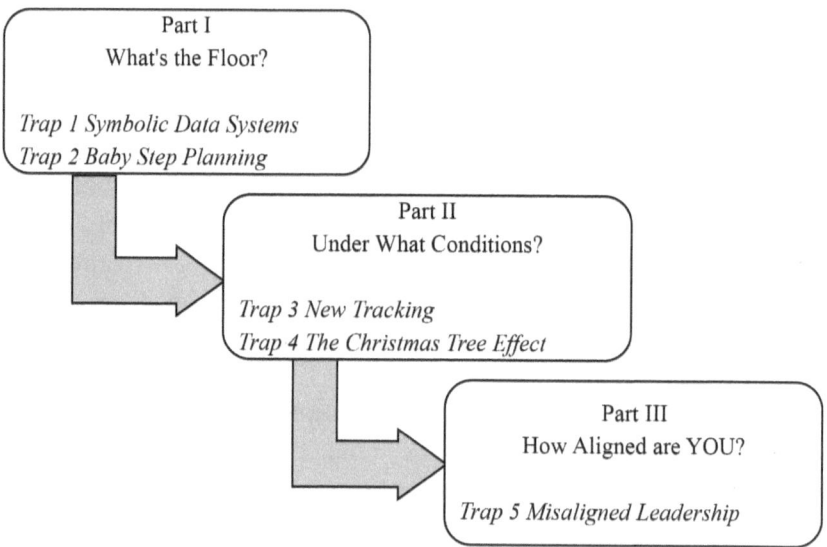

**Figure I.1** Structure of the Book

INTRODUCTION

real-world experiences—the good; the bad; the funny; and, shall we say, the others.

These stories are directly from the schools and districts we have studied. The stories in the chapters are true, though names are changed and stories are sometimes a mash-up of more than one school or district. We took literary license to ensure the privacy of individuals, schools, and districts, as well as for emphasis of the focal points of each chapter. Each chapter elucidates one common systemic inequity trap and provides a practical solution for each.

## PART I: WHAT'S THE FLOOR?

This is the beating heart of the book. It is about how beliefs and expectations about students' capacity to achieve seep into every part of a school system by way of policies and practices. These beliefs and expectations express themselves in insurmountable obstacles for historically lower-achieving students. Chapters 1 and 2 describe how beliefs and expectations result in two of the most common systemic inequity traps that constrain the future for all students.

- "Chapter 1: Symbolic Data Systems" demonstrates the need for equity leaders to be vigilant about the common data practices meant to a promote what is *true, right,* and *just* education for all students. Absent the clarity about the academic expectation for every student, these practices can do more harm than good. The chapter describes the characteristics of the effective data systems for accelerating student success.

- "Chapter 2: Baby-Steps Planning" demonstrates how a school's or district's approach to planning is a clear view into underlying organizational beliefs and expectations about the capacity of all student groups to excel academically. Planning approaches have a direct correlation to the rate of success for historically underachieving students. This chapter contrasts the most common educational planning process and offers an alternative approach that inevitably accelerates student learning.

Introduction

## Part II: Under What Conditions?

The next two chapters discuss two systemic inequity traps that are considerably more difficult to see with the naked eye. This section discusses two of the most prevailing practices intended for adults with the tools to help historically lower-achieving students. This section will demonstrate precisely how these common practices backfire.

- "Chapter 3: New Tracking" is an unexpected twist on an old theme. The chapter details how the historic practice of labeling and sorting of students by demographic group creep back into current education systems with devastating consequences. This chapter details an effective alternative to grouping lower-achieving students together for extended periods of time—one that absolutely accelerates student success.

- "Chapter 4: The Christmas Tree Effect" is an example of one of the most common ways many school systems express their sincere desire to help students—program shopping. The focus of this very honest chapter is on a less obvious reason for this institutional behavior, the impact it has on equity leaders and students, and how to address it.

## Part III: How Aligned are You?

This part contains the systemic inequity trap that is the most overlooked, most inequity producing, and most injurious to life options for African American, Latino, Native American, Pacific Islander, poor, LGBTQ, and other students who may be in vulnerable educational circumstances. This last chapter describes the number one most common systemic inequity trap, as identified through our study of studies.

- "Chapter 5: Misaligned Leadership" is a raw, sobering, and honest treatment of equity leadership that is rarely discussed or shared in an appropriate and respectful manner. The philosophical, dispositional, and behavioral misalignment of key leaders in a school system is a nonstarter, regardless of how earnest the intent of individuals in a school or district. The chapter describes how to address leadership challenges and set up a leadership system that ramps-up student success.

The conclusion of the book offers closing arguments and a heartfelt wish for the future of education for historically lower-achieving students. Finally, for those so inclined, the appendix outlines the methodology we used for what we describe here as the study of studies.

## WHAT MAKES THIS BOOK IMPORTANT?

It is true, right, and just that educators and education advocates insist on equitable school systems because *everyone's child* deserves the premium education that only some student groups have historically experienced, as a matter of course.

This book offers answers to some of the most daunting questions of the day that haunt equity-driven educational leaders everywhere:

- What are the specific structures and practices in schools and districts most associated with advantaging some students and disadvantaging other groups of students?
- Why do most schools and districts implement "research-based" programs but still experience persistent gaps between student groups?
- What must we believe, understand, know, and do differently to successfully lead equity initiatives that authentically accelerate academic success and close historic and persistent student outcome gaps?

We recognize that this book, like the last, will probably be used for book studies, as well as individual reflection. To facilitate these experiences, this book adds a new feature. Readers can access *online actionable tools* that accompany each chapter, with a variety of opportunities to interact with the ideas, including:

- self-assessments

- reflective exercises
- guiding templates

We hope this book adds value to your personal and professional lives. We wrote it for you with all our hope, love, and respect.

### *A Note About the Word Equity*

We recognize the differences of opinion and degrees of emotion triggered by the word *equity* at this moment in history. We use the term *equity* in this book along with "a premium education for all students," and "a true, right, and just education." We ask that educators apply their leadership acumen and use whatever term is best in their context to describe the basic measure of the fairness of a school system. We believe that the urgency to provide all students with the opportunity to reach the highest educational attainment levels, as well as to (finally) close long-standing achievement gaps, supersedes the specific word choice.

# Chapter 1

# Symbolic Data Systems

*Equity Hook: The Emperor's New Clothes*

Have you ever wondered

- if practices around assessment and data really make a meaningful difference to student achievement;
- why people seem not to notice that the outcome gaps between historically struggling student groups and grade level achievement are not closing very much; or
- how it is that historically-struggling students have not made substantial progress despite all the data-driven, progress-monitoring practices popularized the last decade?

One of the most prevalent and gripping systemic inequity traps identified through our study of studies is that of *symbolic data systems*. These refer to units of information and sets of procedures that

- are in place in most schools and districts;
- entail lots of work by many people;
- are directives that must be followed;
- do not necessarily answer practical questions;
- have nominal impact on student achievement; and yet
- enjoy great popularity.

In other words, symbolic data systems exist because people think they are supposed to have them. In practice these systems are more for show than impact. Equity leaders who doubt the efficacy of their school or district assessment and data systems (such as certain practices around benchmark assessments, diagnostic student testing, or some mandated but redundant practices) often experience what the townspeople did in a familiar parable.

### THE EMPEROR'S NEW CLOTHES

As a refresher, the most popular version of the story is about a pair of charlatans who know that their king cares about vanity and fashion above all else. So they tell him that they sew the loveliest garments ever constructed. In fact, their fabric is so special that it can only be seen by people worthy of high status in society. The weavers pretend to work for days and then present the king with his completed "outfit."

The king does not really see the clothes but pretends to, so as to not be considered a fool not worthy of his station. The royal has no choice but to lead a pre-planned parade around his kingdom in his regal new garb, though he is actually in his undergarments! The townspeople, who also do not want their status questioned, rave about the beautiful outfit the king is donning. Only an innocent child calls out the obvious, that the emperor has no clothes! Realizing the truth, the crowd bursts into guffaws. To protect himself from embarrassment, the king awkwardly continues pretending to proudly parade around the town, strutting all the way.

Instead of "The emperor has no clothes!" *the first most common equity hook* is the lost voice in the crowd saying, "Our data system has no impact!" Behaving as if a system has a meaningful impact when it does not is like pretending the emperor has luxurious new clothes when he is actually in his boxers! This example is much more than folly or simply poor practice. A symbolic data system is irrefutably a systemic inequity trap, completely within the control of schools and districts, impeding historically lower-achieving students from reaching the highest rungs of the academic ladder.

*Symbolic data systems always perpetuate, often exacerbate, and sometimes originate the life-altering outcome gaps among historically lower-achieving student groups.*

This was a truth that one district learned in a painful way.

Radiant Unified School District (RUSD) was a special district. It was a high-achieving school district that served almost equal numbers of African American, White, and Latino students, a large portion of whom were from lower-income families. A succession of two long-term superintendents led the district for almost twenty years. Dr. Darling, the first of those superintendents, wrote the official district motto: "RUSD: Where everyone achieves." However, the common language that best characterized the district was "No students get a better education than we provide our students."

During those years one belief was clear across the entire district and wider community. RUSD produced great students. School was about achievement, plain and simple. The district focused on exceptional teaching, powerful learning, and every type of support necessary for students to meet or exceed grade level achievement. Not to be outdone by any district anywhere, music and the arts were part of a well-rounded education at RUSD. The district connected everything to academic goals, even enrichment. Dr. Aliyah, the second of the long-term superintendents, often used this example with students: "If you want to learn fractions, study an instrument. And if you want to be a musician, study fractions."

District leaders felt proud, knowing they educated their students at the highest levels. They did their work intensely and steadily. They frequently referenced their strategy for ensuring that all students excel academically. The strategy began by answering one fundamental question: "What is our floor?"

## What's Your Floor?

This is one of the *most powerful questions* for leaders who are determined to shatter systemic inequities. The answer to this question defines expectations. The term *floor* is used but not at all to connote that the expectation is a low one. Rather, the floor is that absolute, nonnegotiable, applicable-to-every-student, academic level that is expected of every student.

The reason it is such a powerful question is because, as our study of studies demonstrates, almost any district who has *not succeeded* at closing student outcome gaps has *not defined* a clear academic floor for all students. The converse is true for successful districts. Many school systems have *implied* floors that, in practice, are higher for some student groups and lower for others. Not surprisingly, the differences in these expectations directly correlate to historic variations in student achievement levels.

Many school systems have vision and mission statements that generally describe what they want for students—but not a clear floor. These statements sound like the following: "Our district prepares every student to reach their *potential* and become a productive citizen" or "We provide safe supportive environments and innovative opportunities for student learning, promote individual student excellence, invite collaboration and discovery, and challenge students to take responsibility as members of a diverse, global community." For advocates of a premium education for every student, these broad statements are problematic in several ways.

First, there is the equity language translation of the word *potential*. In *Shattering Inequities* (Avelar La Salle and Johnson 2018), we discuss how language is a window into belief systems. Stop a moment and consider the word "potential." The word *potential* assumes an underlying belief that students come to school with a predetermined end to their academic success. That belief is antithetical to establishing a common floor for all students.

For instance, "We help our students reach their potential" is sometimes said to explain the success of a high-achieving student. However, the same phrase is used as rationale for the lack of success of students from historically lower-achieving groups. In this case, the word *potential* plays into the belief that not all students are equally capable of high academic pursuits (often by demographic group). Without a clear delineation of one expectation for every student, the floor is a moving target. Whether by design or naivete, history demonstrates that expectations tend to move up for White students, some Asians, or students from higher-income families. They move down for African American, Latino, and

Indigenous students, as well as groups of students from lower-income families.

The floor is also lower for students in vulnerable circumstances, like those in the foster care system, incarcerated youth, and students with insecure housing. Rarely is it an individual educator's conscious decision to do harm. However, *we are all mere mortals.* As such, we internalize impressions about individuals and groups of people. Subconsciously, this results in decisions that advantage some student groups and disadvantage others. In aggregate, these impressions ubiquitously creep into school systems and impact student futures.

## What Was the Floor for Radiant Unified?

RUSD had a long-standing systemwide floor, impervious to individual beliefs or expectations about students or to the whims of the times. The administrators and staff pointed to clarity of their floor as a major reason

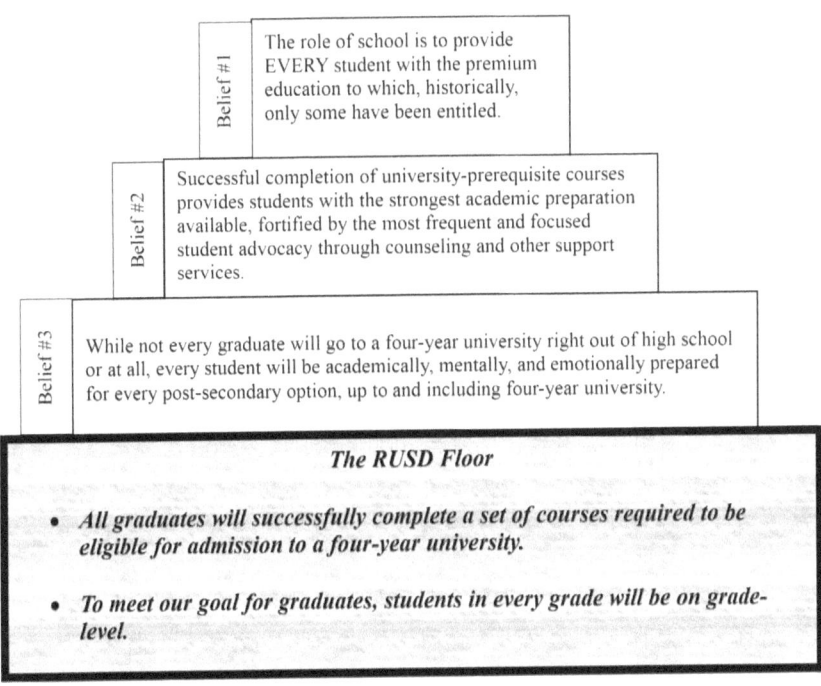

**Figure 1.1** The RUSD Academic Floor

for their success with historically lower-achieving students. Figure 1.1 displays their core beliefs and the RUSD floor that drove their success.

The floor was so clear that even students and parents recited it. "University prepped and on grade level" was the guiding phrase in every district department, every school, and by students at every grade. Nothing was as charming as a kindergartener answering, "So, Hakim, what is your reason for going to school?" In his own, five-year-old pronunciation, Hakim answered, "To be uni-varsity pwepped and on gwade level."

Some would ask, "Are these student recitations meaningful since students may not fully understand what they were saying?" Almost every employee in the district believed that rituals like these did matter because they created a culture of high expectations across the district. Why did the adults feel so proud in reciting their floor for students? A second powerful question made it possible to answer that question with confidence.

### How Do We Know?

How well are students doing? It would be difficult for noneducators to believe, but very often school systems have difficulty answering that question with clarity and conviction. Instead, responses sound like the following actual district statements. Do they sound familiar?

- "Students are improving steadily every year."
- "The district has done a phenomenal job at supporting all students."
- "We are on the cusp of making great strides."

Often, the discussion of the academic floor is simply not the focus of discussions. Instead, responses to the question about expectations for every student include the following:

- "We are trying so hard, but our students have so many challenges that we must focus on their general well-being over achievement."

- "We know our students need help, but we must get it together as adults first."

Here is an unscientific, yet telling experiment to see whether common agreement exists about how students are doing across a school system. Find a group of kindergarten teachers, and their school and district administrators, and ask them, "How many sight words should kinder students know by the end of the year?" Then sit back and marvel at their responses!

We have attended many a board meeting where the district data person shares a comprehensive presentation of achievement in a lengthy, graph-laden, table-riddled, and brilliantly color-coded slideshow. Then at the "any-questions" portion ending the exposition, a barrage of questions comes from the board and community members asking one thing: "Yes, but how are our students doing?"

Many district data leaders discreetly complain to one another about their exasperation over the lack of data expertise of the people asking questions even after detailed explanations. "They never get what I'm saying, no matter how I present it!" That is a true statement. However, the problem is not with the audience. It is not even a problem with the data leader's presentation. Most often, the problem is that, in the absence of a clear achievement floor, results are shared in a dense, convoluted data presentation with a complicated story and an unclear ending.

Often, data leaders have myriad reports accessible to them, and they present them in a long series of independent snapshots. Contrast that with RUSD, where the data presentations were grounded in answering one basic question: How well have students achieved the floor (by demographic group)? Then the RUSD presentations shared a data story that demonstrated how they knew how well students were meeting that floor.

## How Close Were RUSD Students to the District Achievement Floor?

As a standard practice, RUSD leaders shared a specific set of data points they used to monitor their students' academic progress toward the RUSD floor. The data points they shared responded to specific questions asked

**Table 1.1** Annual Achievement Questions and Typical Answers

| Questions | What Progress-Monitoring Data Will Answer? | End-of-Year Answers |
|---|---|---|
| 1. **Can first graders read?** (Juel 1988) | a. Sight words<br>b. Decoding and spelling of nonsense words (phonemic awareness)<br>c. Fluency with comprehension | 85% or more of first graders read on grade level or above, with the same result for all White, Black, and Latino groups. |
| 2. **Can third graders read?** (Fletcher and Lyon 1998) | | 80% or more of third graders read on grade level or above, with the same result for all three major demographic groups. |
| 3. **Are fifth graders proficient in math?** (Siegler and Chen 2012) | a. Division<br>b. Fractions | Almost 80% or more of fifth graders were on grade level or above in math, including White and Black students. Latino students achieved 10% below other groups but 15% above state average for all students. |
| 4. **Are tenth graders proficient in algebra?** (Agustin and Agustin 2009) | a. Factoring*<br>b. Rational functions*<br>*Essential foundational concepts to advanced math | By the end of the tenth grade, 75% of students ended the year proficient or above in algebra, including White and Black students. Latino students performed 15% below other groups but 10% above the state average for all students. |

| | | |
|---|---|---|
| 5. **Are graduating seniors eligible for admission to a four-year university?** (Carnevale et al. 2019) | Grade-specific predictors of graduate success. Depending on the grade, a combination of the following:<br><br>A Combination of These for All Secondary Grades<br>a. Attendance<br>b. Discipline<br>c. State exam result<br>d. Grade point average<br>e. School affiliation<br><br>High School–Only Additions<br>f. University prerequisite courses on track for satisfactory completion<br>g. Correct course placement<br>h. Acceptable grades<br>i. University admissions exam taken<br>j. Completion of federal financial aid application<br>k. Submission of application to post-secondary education option (university, military, high-paying job training, etc.) | 70% of students graduated as four-year university eligible and on grade level or above—there was only a 5% total range in the average results for White, Black, and Latino students. |

by the superintendent and board at the end of each school year. They were *feedback* to the system. Because RUSD was "where everyone achieves," the district collected logical information to answer the questions about where students achieved compared to the district floor. For high-level purposes like board and community meetings, the superintendents shared a subset of the data that told a clear and succinct story about student achievement.

Table 1.1 displays that short list of questions, the RUSD progress-monitoring data system, and the end-of-year responses. Many equity leaders will recognize the wisdom motivating these five specific questions because they represent the short list of well-known predictors of long-term academic success. These five data questions are particularly important for equity leaders to monitor, particularly when serving historically struggling students.

The district focused on setting up a way to ensure that the data they collected led to impactful action. They understood how busy people were, so they set up *data rituals*. These are routines that are calendared ahead of the entire year, set up to ensure that data collection leads directly into agreements that trigger actions intended to improve student outcomes between check points. Dr. Darling was known for saying, "If our data system does not answer the questions *we* pose about our students' success and if it does not trigger actions that *we* take in response, then it is just too much trouble!" But here is the challenge: How do you get an entire school system to

- ask meaningful questions and use data to answer them; and
- most importantly, modify individual adult and systemic practices to create conditions designed to accelerate student achievement, especially for historically struggling students?

*Data Rituals*

Here is an important consideration for designing an impactful data system that provides meaningful and actionable feedback to a school system: we must anticipate what is likely to go wrong and put in "guard rails," or structured routines, to make sure that at least those anticipated challenges are prevented *by design*.

For example, data are valuable if they provide feedback to the various units in a school system, and trigger actions that result in positive change. Therefore, *team collaboration around data* is the point. The data ritual described next is designed to ensure that the point of data use is to provide teams with information they can digest together to make actionable agreements aimed at getting to $X$, where demographics no longer predict achievement.

## RUSD's Data Ritual

The following outlines a systemic ritual that RUSD used to ensure that their data system was meaningful. It should be somewhat familiar to many educators.

- Grade-level or course-alike teacher teams chunked the year into practical units of instructional time, usually about six units of twenty-five teaching days each. (Important note: The more the students were struggling, the more frequently progress was monitored. Twenty-five teaching days is a recommended average unit length for the typical struggling student. This is because the longer the assessment interval, the greater the likelihood that students fall behind without being noticed, and the harder it is to get students up to the expected floor.)
- They then determined which short set of instructional targets they would focus on during each unit.
- Teacher teams created common assessments, pegged to an external determiner of appropriate rigor.
- Then teacher teams reviewed the results after each common assessment during prescheduled data reflection sessions (DRS).
- The DRS ended with a common understanding of what area and which students needed specialized support. Then teams made common agreements about what they would implement during the next unit to help students improve results on the subsequent assessment.
- Discussion of the results of the next common assessment demonstrated how the agreements were implemented and if they were effective.

Here is a critical takeaway. In our decades of experience, almost every school and district that use a similar systemic data ritual at *every level* of the nested system move the students toward *X marks the spot*. This is true especially for historically lower-achieving students. Conversely, most districts that only have data rituals only at the teacher level, which is the most common version of this ritual, make moderate or no progress.

## WHAT IS A NESTED DATA SYSTEM?
### Nested Data System

A nested data system is an orchestrated set of data rituals implemented in succession at every level of a school district. It is designed to make it very *difficult* for students *not* to get to X. The design repurposes one set of data for use by every level in a school system. This reduces the need for assessments to the smallest number with the greatest practical value. Figure 1.2 displays the levels of data analysis and action that comprise the nested data system, beginning from the smallest unit in the center (the individual teacher or counselor) to the outside ring (the district office).

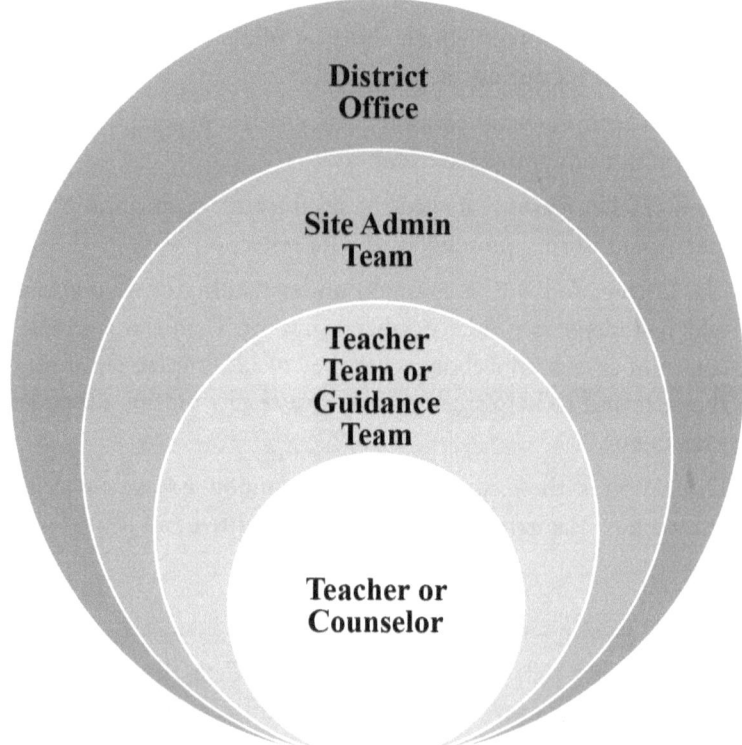

**Figure 1.2** Levels of the Nested Data System

Here is a basic truth regarding one of the uses of the nested data system. The integrity of the data system is paramount. To set the conditions for that integrity, superintendents, district administrators, and site leaders must manage the system to ensure that data are used as a *flashlight*, not a *torch!* This means that the purpose of the data system must be to provide actionable feedback to every level of a school system, nothing directly or indirectly hurtful to staff or students.

The safer educators feel sharing their data,

- the more the data will be accurate;
- the more meaningful the feedback will be at all levels of the school system;
- the more invested people will be in making and keeping agreements about what they will do at each level to improve student results next time; and
- the more profound the outcomes will be for students.

Sometimes consciously (mostly subconsciously) but without fail, people respond to cognitive threat in some way that deflects energy from the goal. In this case, the goal is to make changes in the system that will propel students *toward X*. The data system must be designed to avoid perceived threat to adults in order to have a meaningful impact on students.

This nested data ritual is so effective that it is a hallmark of almost every school or district that makes consequential strides toward getting *all students* to *X*. The complete nested data ritual proceeds in the following manner:

- Common assessments provide *teachers* with feedback on whether students learned what teachers intended them to learn.
  - Individual teachers review their own class data by student and student demographic groups.
- Common assessments provide *teacher teams* (grade level or course alike) with feedback on whether students learned what the team intended.

- Teams review grade-level or course data for individual students and student demographic groups.

- *Site administrative teams* review the results of common assessments for feedback on how their own efforts as site administrators impacted individual teachers; teacher teams; and, ultimately, students.

  - Site administrative teams review data for each of the teacher teams across the school.

- *District office staff* review the results of common assessments for feedback on how their efforts as district office leaders impacted individual schools and, ultimately, students.

  - District office leaders review data for each of the schools across the district.

This ritual is also very effective at providing feedback to middle school and high school counselors, guidance teams, site leadership teams, and district administrators. This application provides feedback about the impact of school guidance supports on the greatest predictors of student success in a premium educational program (as described in Table 1.1). For example, for ninth graders, the greatest predictors include attendance; discipline; grade-point average; placement in grade-appropriate premium courses; and student affiliation with a school group, club, or sport.

In contrast, eleventh-grade predictors include expected grade-appropriate course placement, grades of C or better in those courses, completion of a college entrance exam, and submission of the federal financial aid application. Using the nested data ritual, individual counselors, guidance teams, site administrators, and district office leaders review student progress as a unit to determine whether students are on or off track. They also check in each of the indicators individually to look for underlying reasons for students being on or off track. They do this about five or six times a year in a nested system, triggering agreements about what action steps adults will take at every level, between each checkpoint, to move students toward $X$.

Table 1.2 Anticipated Challenges and Systemic Solutions for Nested Data Systems

| What Could Go Wrong | Data Ritual Systemic Solutions | Person Responsible |
|---|---|---|
| The intended users of the system may not value the assessments intended to provide progress check data. | Every teacher or counselor involved in the progress checks should be part of developing their assessments, in grade-level, course-alike, or counseling teams. | District office administration, in collaboration with principals and teacher/counselor leaders<br>*Tip*: Honor the maxim, "Only the people who participate in the design of assessments value those assessments." |
| The number of progress monitoring assessments may be too infrequent to enable every member of the nested system to identify and help struggling students before they get too far behind to catch up before the next unit of time. | Apply the following recommendations:<br>• Twenty-five days between grade-level or course-level progress checks for the average struggling student (about five assessments before the end of the year). | District office administration, in collaboration with principals and teacher/counselor leaders<br>*Tip*: Commit to one system of progress checks, and eliminate the rest. Layering assessments becomes symbolic to adults and does not yield results for students. |
| Teachers or counselors may not assess students in time for teams at every level to meet to analyze data and agree on between-unit actions to affect next unit student achievement. | Prior to the school year starting, establish and publish a systemwide calendar of the assessment windows and team data-reflection sessions. Conduct a data check two days prior to reflection sessions to see if anything is missing. | District office administration, in collaboration with principals<br>*Tip*: Have one district administrator be the point person for everything related to the calendar. |

*(Continued)*

Table 1.2 Continued

| What Could Go Wrong | Data Ritual Systemic Solutions | Person Responsible |
|---|---|---|
| Teams at every level could have difficulty finding time to meet on a regular basis or staff may find it objectionable to meet outside the school day. | A published calendar for the year of all DRSs, for every level, can be shared at the beginning of the year. Develop a team of guest teachers (substitutes) for each school that could release teacher grade-level or course-alike teams on a rotating schedule. They could release about three teams a day, for 90–120 minutes each. | Human resources administrator at the district, in collaboration with principals *Tip*: A best practice is to have one team of guest teachers assigned to a set group of schools. Also, guest teachers can provide specialty lessons that serve as applied academics, like music, art, physical education, coding, or another interesting use of technology. Expanded Day providers can also be used creatively to fill this role. |
| DRS discussions and agreements could become generic and not focus sufficient attention on the degree of learning by different groups of vulnerable students. | Design a discussion protocol with questions that ask about achievement by student demographics (racial, ethnic, language minority, socioeconomic, housing insecure, foster status, LGBTQ+), class or program participation, or any other grouping possibly correlated to specific student groups or individuals. Include a space for action agreement for each group profile discussed. | DRS facilitators *Tip*: At first, a lot of time is spent on searching the data for the answer to the protocol questions. The goal, however, is to become fluent at that step so that more of the allotted time is spent on making action agreements to be implemented between units. Then, each subsequent DRS begins with a self-evaluation of how well the agreements had the desired effect on student achievement. |

| DRS discussions could occur too long after the next unit has started. This means that the new unit is well underway when the DRS occurs, therefore reducing the amount of targeted time the team has to implement agreements aimed at improving outcomes for the upcoming unit. | Tune up district data capabilities to enable assessments to be scored and results to be available very soon after actual assessment administration. | District data officer<br><br>*Tip*: To have maximum relevance to participants at every level, DRSs should be able to occur no later than three days after assessment administration. |

Here is a blinking yellow caution light. As we wrote in *Shattering Inequities*, "love is in the details," and this data system is effective only if implemented with technical care (Avelar La Salle and Johnson 2018). Otherwise, it can have elements that seem right, but still be only symbolic and ineffectual. Table 1.2 lists some of the most anticipated issues that make a data system more symbolic than meaningful to historically lower-achieving students, and it provides some practical solutions for each.

## WINDSTORM IN THE FORECAST FOR RUSD

Even though their data systems were sophisticated and well-practiced, RUSD was jarred by hard times. COVID hit. Schools closed. Then they opened. Then they partially closed again. Then they opened one more time. New thinking swept over federal, state, and local politics, and eventually, the district felt like it was in the eye of a hurricane. The second of the long-term superintendents retired, and a new majority on the board of education was elected on the platform that their district needed change.

They wanted innovation, specialty-branded schools, technology everywhere, and business partnerships for every campus. They wanted events that captured the attention of the media. The new board believed that their existing motto was old-fashioned. They hired a new superintendent who agreed with them on all counts and, after engaging a large group of district and community representatives, replaced the old motto with a new one.

- Old motto—"RUSD: Where everyone achieves."
- New motto—"We graduate each student with the technical, problem-solving, academic, social and emotional, and entrepreneurial skills needed to fulfill their potential and become champions of their own success in a future that does not yet exist."

This new vision transformed the district culture surprisingly swiftly. It used to be that everyone united around doing everything necessary for every student to reach the same high level of achievement, getting to *X marks the spot*. It became an organization with two distinct groups. One group of leaders vocally championed the new direction, no matter the issue. They shared that the new direction was fresh. As it happened, most of these leaders were newer to the district, having joined within the previous five years or so. They also quietly felt that supporting the new direction represented job security, given the new district politics. These leaders became the "in-house" group. The employee associations staunchly supported these leaders because of the "professional freedom" that came with the new district stance.

The other group of leaders questioned parts of the new direction and, for that reason, received the monikers of recalcitrant or obsolete. If the first group were called the "in-house" leaders, you can imagine the informal label ascribed to the second group!

## WHAT DID THE OUT-OF-FAVOR LEADERS QUESTION?

Most of the not-in-house leaders who had concerns were those who were part of the twenty-year tenure of the two long-term superintendents. This second group of leaders lived the jolt that came with the first superintendent's arrival twenty years prior. They lived through the storming that preceded the clarity that RUSD was about graduating university-eligible and academically prepared students. They lived through the initial phase of using data to help students, clumsy and imperfect though it was. Then, over time, they experienced the growing and undeniable success that came from years of trial and error.

This second group of leaders became resistant primarily because, two decades prior to this time, they'd experienced the mistakes that the new district administration and board were repeating. Since then, they'd developed a keen eye for the difference between data systems that were more symbolic and those data with the technical and practical integrity to meaningfully serve as accelerants to *get students to X*.

Were these just contrarian principals? Table 1.3 lists their concerns and their reasoning about what made the new direction for data use merely symbolic. After reviewing this table, you decide whether this group of leaders were causing conflict for conflict's sake, or whether their critiques had merit.

**Table 1.3** Symbolic Data System Elements

| Concerns That the Data System was Merely Symbolic | Rationale for Concern |
| --- | --- |
| Not having a clearly communicated achievement floor | Inequities live when there is a lack of systemwide calibration on expectations for student achievement for all students. In the absence of a clear floor, what replaces it are harmful adult (and student) belief systems and expectations about inherent differences in the capacities of students from different demographic groups to reach the highest academic levels. |
| Infrequent assessments—in this case, one at the beginning of the year, one after winter break, and one the last month of school | Meaningful assessment data provides frequent and systemic feedback about how well students learned what was intended *in time* to do something about it. The art is in deciding how frequently students should be assessed to provide timely feedback in a practical way, without being intrusive on instruction. The principle is that the more the students are struggling, the more frequent should be their progress checks. By any measure, assessing twice prior to the end of the year (as in this case) has the effect of appearing to have an assessment system but has no meaningful way to help students *get to X*. |
| Administering commercial benchmarks that are independent of teacher team plans for intended learning | "How well did students learn what teachers taught?" Answering this is the most meaningful reason to assess students so that immediate action is possible to change conditions and improve student achievement. The bottom line is that assessments must match intended learning targets, not the reverse. |
| Data reflection session (DRS) discussions that are optional and have no expected structure | "If you expect it, you must inspect it" (Avelar La Salle and Johnson 2018). Optional direction is received as unimportant and will be taken by a select few members of any organization. In essence, making structured DRSs optional makes them systemically meaningless. |

SYMBOLIC DATA SYSTEMS

| | |
|---|---|
| Assessment results that are available two weeks after students took the assessments | For assessment results to have impact, interested parties at every level of a system must know that feedback will come immediately after the assessment is given to students. Otherwise, the results become obsolete and do not inspire immediate and coordinated action toward making changes to effect improvements on the next assessment. |
| Assessment results reported to the board that compare schools and admonish principals | This is the kiss of death. Any data meant for an external audience cease to become meaningful, actionable feedback. This practice can actually harm students. |

Notice that many of their concerns came directly from the anticipated challenges outlined in table 1.2. You may also notice how subtle some of the differences are between the practices proposed by the new district leaders and those supported by the previous administration. These seemingly small, inconsequential differences can mean the difference between success and continued struggle for historically lower-achieving students.

### *One Degree Delta ($1°Δ$)*

"One degree delta" is a phrase to describe the nature of the concerns raised by that second group of principals. It is a caution that the wrong modifications, even tiny ones (referred to as a "one degree of difference from an intended design," or simply, $1°Δ$), compromise the integrity of any practice and often have long-term effects on student achievement.

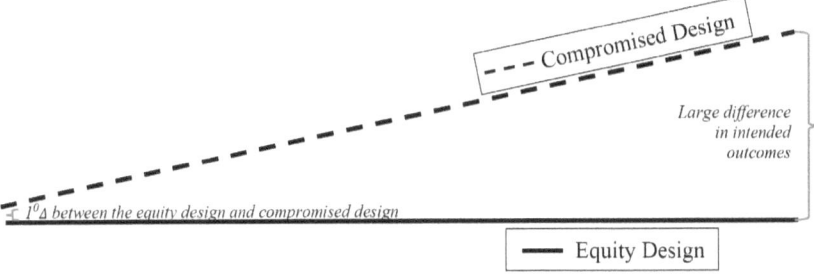

**Figure 1.3** One Degree Delta

The concerns and rationale the principals raised in table 1.3 came from years of honing their data system. During those two decades, they learned that seemingly inconsequential compromises made early on can make huge differences in student outcomes over time. As an example, figure 1.3 graphically represents $1^0\Delta$ related to the effectiveness of data systems to *get students to X*.

During this new chapter of the RUSD story, the board and superintendent reported that their new initiatives "enhanced the good things the district had been doing." So, to the public, the district used to have a strong progress monitoring and data system, and the district planned to continue it. However, to fit the pressures of the new direction, the district leadership allowed changes that seemed insignificant at the time. To the leaders who were part of the learning along the way, the changes listed in table 1.3 were compromises that they knew would be detrimental to students.

## RUSD after the New Direction

This story is sad but true. Just one year after the new direction, RUSD student achievement declined. This decline became a trend for the next five years. Achievement for all student groups suffered, except for one. The small group of students from higher-income families declined a small amount, not by much, and they were still above grade level. In the end the difference in achievement gaps for the other groups doubled. Results from the year-end state assessment demonstrated that

- the gap between lower-income White students and the higher-income group grew from 15 percent to 30 percent, further behind grade level; and
- the gap between the African American and Latino student groups, compared to that of the higher-income group, grew from 20 percent to 40 percent, also further behind grade level.

Lest we leave readers with a heavy heart, there is one more piece to this story. As RUSD achievement decreased, surrounding districts began to improve their data systems, and make positive gains. The local newspapers got ahold of the story and pointed out the contrast between the achievement decline in RUSD that had previously posted positive annual gains, and the increases in surrounding districts. Community pressure resulting from the negative press caused some RUSD leaders moving to other districts, though the superintendent chose to stay. Half of the board members remained, while the other half moved on.

By now, both the superintendent and the board realized that something was very, very wrong. And now the newer district office administration solicited the experience and training of those leaders who were concerned that the data system was more symbolic than substantive. Not all the leaders from that original group were still in the district, but the voices of those who remained became prominent.

The district is not where it once was. That cannot be sugarcoated. However, they are moving in a positive direction and are recommitted to designing a district-wide data system that will promote a premium education for every student so that all student groups can get to *X marks the spot*.

## Summary

Chapter 1 describes the first of the most common systemic inequity traps identified though our study of studies—symbolic data systems. Schools and districts that serve historically lower-achieving students often fall into this trap, where student assessment and data analysis structures are installed but are more symbolic than substantive. Akin to the lesson in the familiar story, "The Emperor's New Clothes," some equity leaders clearly see the limitations of many current practices but hesitate to verbalize concerns for fear of being ostracized.

This was the case in Radiant Unified, a district that was once a beacon of educational justice for having all student groups *get to X*, the place where demographics no longer predict achievement. But after two decades, RUSD students eventually succumbed to the harmful effects of a data system that morphed into something in vogue, but which was largely symbolic and legally compliant. The chapter begins with the premise that defining a clear expectation for all students, setting the academic "floor," is a prerequisite to reversing historic disparities in educational attainment by demographic groups. This chapter highlights the harmful effects on students of seemingly minute, inconsequential compromises to data systems—maybe only one degree different ($1^0\Delta$) from the intended design.

## Equity Concepts

- "What is the floor?"—It is that absolute, nonnegotiable academic goal that applies to every student. It must be communicated throughout the school system and then monitored to ensure that everyone's actions align to *getting to X*, which is the major reason for the existence of schools and districts.

- Nested data system—It is a data collaboration design for making data actionable at *every level* of a school system, making it difficult for all students *not* to succeed.

- Data rituals—They are routines instituted to make sure that any anticipated challenges to an effective use of data are prevented.

- "One Degree Delta" ($1^0\Delta$)—This is a caution that a small compromise in the integrity of any design, even a one-degree difference, can have long-term effects on student outcomes.

## Actionable Tools

Now it is time for you, readers, to apply the guidance from this chapter to your school systems. Gather a team of leaders. We invite you to engage with online templates to more deeply consider the implications of symbolic data systems in your school or district. Access templates at https://orendaed.org/WhereEquityLives/.

CHAPTER 2

# Baby-Steps Planning

*Equity Hook: Backcast, Don't Forecast*

HAVE YOU EVER WONDERED

- how school systems often meet their student acceleration plan goals, yet students from historically struggling groups are still far behind their more successful peers;
- if anyone else thinks that plan writing is mostly a tedious exercise in legal compliance;
- why planning sometimes feels like a case of people free associating ways to spend money by deadlines so as not to lose it; or
- whether there exists any way to plan that can actually help school systems dedicated to getting students to *X marks the spot*?

One of the most unexpected findings from the study of studies was that something as mundane as "planning" (insert "blah" here!) can be a game changer for getting students to *X*. Many readers are familiar with the phrase "Follow the money" in order to understand what an organization believes and values. In this case, we offer "Follow the planning" to understand institutional beliefs and expectations about students. In one form or another, written school and district plans answer two fundamental equity questions: "Where is *X marks the spot* on the horizon?" and "What's our floor now?" That is, when viewed with *equity vision*, plan documents express the *institutional beliefs* about what different groups of students are capable of achieving. Therein lies their power to help or harm. Here is what we mean.

"Baby-steps" is usually a phrase with a positive connotation. For example, a person might join a gym to get fit, only to feel defeated watching other, more experienced gym-goers accomplish feats that appear impossible. In response, a trainer might say to a novice gym enthusiast, "Baby-steps—you are doing great, you will be able to do a little more each day." There exist times like these when slow, incremental, patient improvement is necessary and appropriate. However, baby-steps planning to correct decades of languishing achievement for entire populations of students is not one of those times.

A truly unexpected insight from our study of studies is that differences in planning perspectives are associated with a great deal of the historic gaps in achievement by different student groups. Naming some of these popular planning approaches would likely create cognitive and emotional distress for those wedded to their processes.

Instead, we will share insights through the story of Marlene. She was a teacher in a very effective school who later became a principal. Her teaching experience in a great school provided her with the understanding of how planning approaches reveal the beliefs and expectations a school has about different groups of students. This perspective influenced her thinking and practice as a principal in ways that fundamentally changed the academic trajectory of her students.

## Teacher Marlene

Teacher Marlene's first assignment out of college was in a magnet school with a unique and very effective model of serving students with learning differences. (One unique characteristic of the school was that teachers were addressed by the title "teacher," followed by their first name.) The Speech and Language Center (SLC) was a reverse-mainstreaming elementary school that specialized in working with students with a variety of labels, including autistic, spectrum disordered, emotionally disturbed, aphasic, and a host of others. The one commonality among these students was that they had speech and language needs, from having moderate delays to being nonverbal. The following describes the structure of the program:

- Every class of twenty students had ten students with learning differences and ten typical learners who served as language role models. Both groups represented all demographics.
- The school did not identify students by labels once they enrolled. Students were socialized to understand that everyone has strengths and areas needing improvement. Therefore, no negative stigma existed for any student.
- Classrooms were multigrade, with students within a range of three years of age.

The school was remarkably effective at helping students with learning differences make unbelievable turnarounds. For example, Jillian enrolled as a four-and-a-half-year-old. She was labeled autistic with "moderate to severe cognitive delays," and as "nonverbal." At the new-student introduction ceremony, she required two adults to help her walk onto the stage, stand in the center while she was introduced, and then walk her off the stage to her seat.

Four years later, Jillian was the student leader who helped new students walk across the stage, *she* introduced them to the audience, and then *she* guided them off the stage, down the stairs, and to their seats in the auditorium. Just about every student at the Speech and Language Center experienced remarkable growth. Their "secret sauce" sounds almost too simple, but here it is.

They decided on a floor and made plans for every student to get there. Their floor was that all students would be on grade level before they left the school after fifth grade. That's it! Educators who work with students with learning differences appreciate how uncommon it is to have the same expectation for all types of learners. Very often, words like *potential* or *growth* are used in goal descriptions for students with disabilities. Rarely is the floor for these students to achieve at least grade level.

CHAPTER 2

## *That* Parent!

At a new-parent orientation, Teacher Marlene shared a profound experience. Her story demonstrated how institutional beliefs about the capacity of students to achieve express themselves in real ways. Teacher Marlene told the new-parent group about an episode with one of her student's parents. About one month after school started, Teacher Marlene received a visit from the mother of her five-year-old student Glenn. The mom was an experienced teacher in another school, so she approached Teacher Marlene with a certain amount of self-assurance and gravitas.

Teacher Marlene was right out of college but had interned at the school for the final two years of her credential program, so she was experienced in the school program. The mom was concerned about the work in her son's backpack. He had incomplete assignments directing him to read and write a list of words that came from the story they read in class. Then he was to draw pictures of what each word meant.

The mom was there to remind Teacher Marlene that her son was nonverbal and did not comprehend language. She said it would be advisable for Teacher Marlene to take baby-steps with Glenn. How could he read and write if he could not understand or use speech? The new parents to the school listened intently and demonstrated body language expressing agreement with the mom's point of view.

Teacher Marlene said she and Glenn's mother "discussed" the school's core belief that all of the students can reach at least grade-level proficiency before they leave the school at the end of the fifth grade. Teacher Marlene tried to get the mom to agree with her that it is impossible to know what *another person* can achieve. That is humanly unknowable.

The school was designed to give students the specialized support they needed to attain the highest academic levels before they left fifth grade. Teacher Marlene designed instructional plans to accelerate Glenn's academic growth that school year in order to reach the high bar five years later. Despite the mother's "counsel," Teacher Marlene was resolute that Glenn would learn to read and write that year. At that point many hands shot up.

## COMING OR GOING?

Rather than answering the questions, Teacher Marlene introduced someone from the audience who she said would answer their questions. Teacher Marlene introduced *that* mom—Glenn's mom! After some nervous chuckles from the parents, Glenn's mom affirmed that everything Teacher Marlene had said about her was true! She revealed that her interactions with Teacher Marlene were probably the most humbling and instructive of her life.

Glenn's mom shared that she was accustomed to defining goals for in her classroom by understanding students' baseline achievement level when they came to her and then planning her year for her class. She expected reasonable improvement during the year and then waited to see how far her students got by the end of the year. To her, any improvement was something to celebrate.

Then Teacher Marlene jumped in and shared that the term for that type of planning is *forecasting*—planning incremental, reasonable, and attainable progress. She explained that SLC plans in reverse, using a process called *backcasting*.

### *Backasting vs. Forecasting*

Backcasting is an approach to planning where a desired future determines decisions about the present. Teacher Marlene explained it like this. Backcasting is like creating your five-year career plan. For example, a group of middle school assistant principals might decide they want to be principals in five years. Based on that goal, they know they need experience at every level and that getting positions at the high school level is hardest of all. So they decide to work up to getting high school assistant principal experience in years three and four. In years one and two, they will apply for elementary assistant principalships since having K–8 experience will make them stronger candidates for the high school assistant principalship. In essence, a goal that is five years away determines plans today, tomorrow, and the next day.

In contrast, forecasting is like a second group of assistant principals with a general career goal to move up. One of them takes a position at the district office coaching new teachers. Another is enticed by a job at the county office of education in charge of special projects. Still another decides to take over compliance for a cluster of schools. And the rest remain in their current positions, waiting to see what happens.

At the end of five years, the first group is quite likely to have a breadth of experience that makes them competitive candidates for a principalship at any level, greatly increasing their odds of landing a post. Absent a specific goal with a fixed endpoint, the career trajectory for the second group is more dubious. Some may become principals in five years, but that will be determined more by chance than by design.

## BACK TO SCHOOL

The way Teacher Marlene thought about goals for Glenn was mind-blowing for his mother. Teacher Marlene asked, "Where would Glenn be by the end of high school, if we set 'realistic and attainable' goals for him each year?" (The phrase "realistic and attainable" to describe student goals is a standard concept in education, generalized from standard practice in special education.) Chills went down Glenn's mom's spine at the epiphany that school systems almost always plan achievement goals for students using this forecasting logic. Imagine how limited her child's goals would be when starting from being nonverbal and not understanding language? His expected growth would be so slow that he would never even graduate from high school, and his life options would be severely limited.

## WHAT ABOUT GLENN?

The mother ended her share by telling the parents that her son stayed at the school for five years. He left the school fully verbal (a few immature phonemes lingered), almost on grade level in every subject, and though a bit lower in writing, he was no different from other students in his class that were originally enrolled in either half of the class. And now, eleven years later, Glenn is a recent college graduate in a professional position, earning $75,000 a year, living a full life (and yes, this is a true story).

Each school year, SLC students exceeded what comparable students achieved in other schools, which is true for both students with learning differences and language role model students. Teacher Marlene experienced the power of the backcasting planning process for the eight years she was at the school. She knew no other way to plan for accelerated achievement.

### Congratulations, Principal Marlene!

Eventually, the district tagged Teacher Marlene to help spread the SLC magic to other schools. She became a program specialist and then coordinator at the district for a few years. Then she accepted the position of assistant principal at an elementary school with 25 percent identified students with disabilities (almost triple the national average). She was distressed because most of those students were achieving in the single digits of grade-level proficiency, but she felt like she was the only person who was worried.

She had high aspirations for changing that picture for her new students, but as assistant principal, she was limited in what she was able to accomplish. When the principal moved on at the end of her second school year, Marlene was appointed principal. She felt so ready! She excitedly went to meet her assistant superintendent of educational services to share her thoughts about how she would begin her work at her new school.

1. Her plan was to bring the staff together for some planning.
   - The assistant superintendent loved the idea.
2. Principal Marlene planned to set the fifth-grade academic floor for every student leaving to middle school.
   - The assistant superintendent loved that idea as well.
3. The principal shared the backcasting process she planned to use, beginning with fifth grade, going down each subsequent grade.
   - The assistant superintended loved that idea even more.
4. Teachers would commit to achievement milestones for chunks of the school year to ensure students were on grade level or above by fifth grade. Principal Marlene and the leadership team would write

the required, school-board-approved, annual school plan based on the achievement targets that came from that process and would then plan their strategies for getting all their students to meet those targets.

- Screech! The assistant superintendent *did not* love that idea.

He took out the district template for school plans and began to explain the district planning process. He explained to Marlene that her school and the district are held accountable to the targets they write into the plans, so the goals needed to be reasonable and attainable, otherwise they would be penalized. As he spoke, Principal Marlene visualized a chart that compared the process she used at SLC with the one her assistant superintendent described.

She realized they were almost the opposite of one another. She wanted to set targets based on the growth rate required to have all fifth graders graduate at least on grade level, no matter how ambitious they were. The assistant superintendent wanted her to set targets based on small, incremental increases determined by the present academic level of her students.

Principal Marlene's approach to planning was backcasting; the district's approach was forecasting. This example illustrates how forecasting often leads to baby-steps goals that create an anchor to the accelerated growth students need to *get to X*.

Our study of studies has demonstrated that utilizing a backcasting planning approach at a systems level yields greatly accelerated outcomes for historically lower–achieving students, yet most districts do not use this approach to systems planning. A challenge is that many plans education leaders are responsible for writing are based on legal requirements, mandated templates, and required processes. Most of these are grounded on a forecasting framework—baby-steps planning.

This makes forecasting the prevailing planning approach, and it is one that leaders rarely question. Recent experiences with COVID provide another example of the differences in decisions and student outcomes that are associated with planning approaches. Recall the funding that was allocated to school districts as a response to pandemic-related school closures.

Funding sources were announced in rapid succession, requiring districts to submit written plans within a very short window and requiring funds to be spent soon after that. While the pandemic created strained situations, it is usual course of business for education leaders to receive disjointed pots of money with requirements that make it very challenging to thoughtfully plan.

Table 2.1 lists some of these pandemic-related funding sources and their requirements. Notice the timelines and imagine (or recall) the weight felt by education leaders trying to do the right thing (California State Department of Education 2022).

The point of table 2.1 is not the amount of funding in response to the pandemic. Educators are grateful for the investment in education during unprecedented times. The table is presented as a timely illustration of the conditions under which school systems often must plan. These are extreme conditions; however, new laws, compliance regulations, funding opportunities, grant awards, and focused donations often present themselves this same way.

They may amount to small or large amounts of money, and there may be more time between spending deadlines, but the challenge is the same for equity leaders. How can equity champions influence the plans for the use of these funds in a way that will get students to $X$? The following is an excerpt from a (spending) plan that resulted from a district feeling pressures of spending deadlines, plan requirements, and a flurry of mandates. Notice the disjointed, incoherent, "free association" nature of the plan. As you read it, ask: What is the design for helping struggling students reach grade-level or beyond?

## DISTRICT FORECASTED PLAN
### *ESSER II*

> *Mathematics workbooks, high school credit recovery, licenses for online texts, online teacher-credential program, language support interventions, literacy acceleration summer, booster curriculum and*

*professional development, purchase and training for intervention curriculum, parent phone-message system, Parent Leadership Training Institute, Family Literacy Program purchase, coaching for staff on socioemotional/behavior health, and teacher professional development on addressing unfinished learning*

## GEER II

*Professional development for high-needs schools, school-based wellness centers, contributing to State School Leadership Institute, and communication to attract new teachers*

## ESSER III

*Cleaning supplies, additional health staff, stipends for COVID testing staff, independent study program materials and supplies, credit recovery program purchase, technology capacity to gather students in a large setting, and intervention curriculum to address learning gaps*

**Table 2.1** US Federal Pandemic-Related Funding Programs

| Funding Sources | Intent | Spending Trigger | Spending Deadline |
|---|---|---|---|
| CARES Act | Learning supports, expanded learning, diagnostic testing, instructional materials, device connectivity, socioemotional supports, professional development, school meals, health testing, and cleaning supplies | 3/2020 | 3/2021 |
| ESSER 1 | Learning supports for lower-achieving students, technology, training and supplies for sanitation, mental health support, expanded learning, local needs, and other activities to continue school operations | 3/2020 | 9/2022 |

| GEER 1 | Learning supports, expanded learning, diagnostic assessments, mental and emotional health services, technology, professional development, meals, and emergency supplies | 3/2020 | 9/2022 |
| --- | --- | --- | --- |
| ESSER II | Addressing learning loss, preparing schools for reopening, and air quality of buildings | 3/2020 | 9/2023 |
| GEER II | Expanded learning, tutoring and other learning-recovery programs, mental and emotional health, technology, credit-deficient students, diagnostic and progress-monitoring assessment, and professional development | 3/2020 | 9/2023 |
| ESSER III SEA- Reserve- Emergency Fund | Expanded learning, tutoring and other learning recovery programs, mental and emotional health, technology, credit-deficient students, diagnostic and progress-monitoring assessment, and professional development | 3/2020 | 9/2024 |
| ESSER III SEAReserve- Learning Loss | Expanded learning, tutoring and other learning recovery programs, mental and emotional health, technology, credit-deficient students, diagnostic and progress-monitoring assessment, and professional development | 3/2020 | 9/2024 |
| ESSER III | Adding public health protocols to above | 3/2020 | 9/2024 |
| EANS II | For schools with high percentage of low-income students | 3/2020 | 9/2024 |
| HYC I | Assistance for homeless students | 3/2020 | 9/2024 |
| HYC II | Assistance for homeless students | 3/2020 | 9/2024 |

This illustration only displays spending plans for three funding sources because that is sufficient to demonstrate the outcome of forecast planning. The true, right, and just question is, How will these plans get students to *X marks the spot*? Looking back on the district plan, one district superintendent lamented, "My goodness. I see that our planning perspective was whatever we saw immediately in front of us. We really never looked out to the horizon to gauge whether our plans would get our students anywhere meaningful. We did not have the time. And honestly, we did not think to plan that way." This is what often occurs with forecast planning.

In contrast, another district planned by using the following backcasting approach.

1. The district team began by defining an eight-year super goal: "Every student will be on grade level or above." Their five-year intermediate goal was "The achievement gap between lower-achieving student group and grade level will be cut by half."
2. Then they plotted all their funding sources onto the calendar as the backdrop of their plan. (For illustration purposes, only the pandemic-related funding sources are shown on figure 2.1.)
3. From there on they focused on the moral imperative to provide every student with a premium education, regardless of the group they represent. To get there, they backcasted without concentrating on the funding sources or amounts.

An important point is that they adopted the stance that as funding came in, it would be plotted according to spending deadlines to fund the actions *they reverse engineered* to get students to *X marks the spot* in eight years.

Figure 2.1 is an example of the calendar this district created to view all funding sources as part of one cohesive eight-year plan to get students to *X*. Each row represents each school year, starting in March, which is when they began refining plans for the following school year. Follow the headings on the first column that say "Year 1," "Year 2," and so forth to identify each school year. Notice that the team highlighted the months of June, July, and August. That is because they identified summer programs as a necessary part of their plan to have student learning grow more than one year for every year in school. This was an essential part of getting their students to *X marks the spot*.

Notice that setting up a backcasting calendar in this manner, from the *end goals* for students, encourages planning from that desired endpoint to the present. Given that supergoal and midpoint milestone, a school system district can now:

| Mar | Apr | May | June | July | Aug | Sept | Oct | Nov | Dec | Jan | Feb |
|---|---|---|---|---|---|---|---|---|---|---|---|
| | | | | Summer Program | | | | | | | |
| Year 1 2020 | | | | | | | | | | 2021 | |
| Year 2 2021 *CARES Act* | | | | | | | | | | 2022 | |
| Year 3 2022 | | | | | | ESSER I GEER I | | | | 2023 | |
| Year 4 2023 | | | | | | ESSER II GEER II | | | | 2024 | |
| Year 5 2024 | | | | Gap ½ | | ESSER III EAN II HYC I, II | | | | 2025 | |
| Year 6 2025 | | | | | | | | | | 2026 | |
| Year 7 2026 | | | | | | | | | | 2027 | |
| Year 8 2027 | | | | X | | | | | | 2028 | |

**Figure 2.1** District Funding Calendar Using Backcasting

1. backcast annual goals for every year and chunks of each year, starting from the eighth year to the end of first year, in that order;

2. identify necessary support (time, training, materials, etc.) for the adults who serve students, plotted from the eighth year to the end of the first;

3. add costs to that support plotted on each row or cell on the calendar, as appropriate; and

4. assign existing funds to pay for those costs and identify any shortfalls.

Now when schools or districts receive unexpected funds or mandates, equity leaders can use the backcasting calendar to facilitate discussions about where those funds best fit their existing plan to get students to

CHAPTER 2

X. The *predetermined future* for students drives the spending. The *need to spend* does not determine the future for students.

## BACK TO PRINCIPAL MARLENE

We want to share that the assistant superintendent revamped the way the district traditionally planned based on his collaboration with Principal Marlene. We want to share that—but alas, it is not so. In fact, the assistant superintendent felt that the district was not ready to take on a change of that magnitude, particularly when the legally required plans were built on a forecasting premise. More than that, the district would be held accountable to the results they set as targets, so making those targets attainable was extremely important. "Baby-steps, Marlene" were the assistant superintendent's final words that meeting.

Principal Marlene pondered the outcome of her district meeting and decided to adopt a long-game strategy. She decided to create two plans—one to turn into the district following their forecasting process and another working plan that was backcasted. Yes, that was double the work, but this is a true story, and such is the life of an equity champion sometimes. Principal Marlene personally lived the powerful impact backcasting had on her students at SLC. She could not imagine denying any of the students at her new school a future with every life option.

Another ending to Principal Marlene's story is that after four years, her school's student achievement came to the attention of the superintendent and the board. Her school profile was trending very differently from that of the district's. The school was closing the gap, impressively heading toward grade-level achievement, while the district was not. Figure 2.2 compares the typical district achievement profiles that tend to result from forecasting versus results from backcasting approaches to planning. Principal Marlene's students were on their way to $X$, while the district gaps persisted.

The district was sincere and working as hard as it could. So when Principal Marlene's student results were noticed, the superintendent sent a delegation of principals and district office leaders to her school to learn from her success. They found many exemplary practices that could be replicated across the district. However, the one that stood out

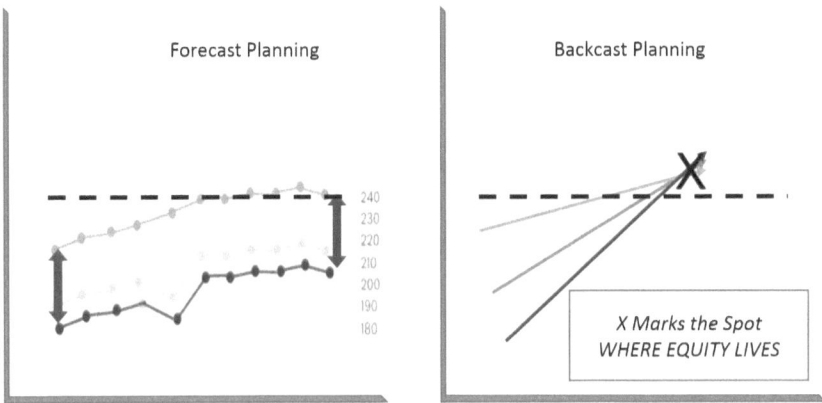

Note: Dashed line represents grade-level achievement. Other lines represent different demographic groups.

**Figure 2.2** Typical Achievement Profiles by Planning Approach

most to the superintendent was the fundamental difference between the district and Principal Marlene: her premise about the capacity of all students to achieve at the highest levels. Marlene explained this as the difference between backcasting and forecasting, and she shared the for-school-eyes-only version of her plan.

The superintendent told the board, "We have been doing a fine job. All our students are growing academically. But if we change nothing, everyone will likely continue to improve, but the gap between our student groups will never close. Teacher Marlene's school shows us that we can do so much better for our historically lower-achieving students."

And so it was that the district eventually adopted backcasting and revamped their planning processes and templates. We would love to share that the district's move toward having all student groups *get to X* received great public attention. In fact, that is exactly what occurred! The district was recognized almost every subsequent year by the state and federal departments of education, as well as the Business Roundtable, as a high minority, high-poverty, high-achieving school district. Almost fifteen years later, the district continues to be a district to watch for their success in accelerating all student groups getting to *X marks the spot where equity lives*!

## Summary

This chapter illustrates the surprising finding that some of the most common planning processes used in education today create powerful systemic inequity traps for historically lower-achieving students. This unexpected finding from our study of studies puts the mundane topic of school and district plans under an equity spotlight that cannot be ignored. In this chapter we meet Teacher Marlene, who learned backcasting, a planning approach quite different from what occurs in most school systems. She did not realize there was any other way to think about planning for student success until she became a principal. As principal, she was directed to use forecasting, a very common planning approach based on a fundamentally different premise about the academic capabilities of student groups. The chapter details the implications for getting students to $X$ if we continue to use the most popular planning approaches used in school systems today.

## Equity Concepts

- Forecasting—This refers to a planning approach that is used most in school systems. Past achievement patterns serve as the baseline from which incremental, reasonable, and attainable goals are derived for the future. Referred to here as baby-steps planning, this approach tends to yield modest goals by design.

- Backcasting—This refers to a planning approach that begins by determining a desired outcome for student achievement in a fixed point of time in the future. Then through a process of reverse engineering, actions needed to accomplish that goal are defined, starting from the fixed future point and moving to the present. This approach tends to yield accelerated goals by design.

## Actionable Tools

Now is the time for you, the readers, to check for baby-steps planning in your own school or district. We invite you and a team to use the online templates to delve more deeply into the implications of baby-steps planning in your school system. Locate them at https://orendaed.org/WhereEquityLives/.

CHAPTER 3

# New Tracking

*Equity Hook: A Rose by Any Other Name*

HAVE YOU EVER WONDERED

- why all our investments in interventions rarely result in high achievement levels for historically lower-performing students;
- if other leaders privately feel as ill-equipped to help historically lower-achieving students; or
- whether it is really possible to provide an educational program strong enough to overcome the out-of-school conditions that impact achievement for many students?

These questions lead us to the next of the most common systemic inequity traps—*new tracking*, aka "a rose by any other name."

Many educators are familiar with the legacy of institutionalized labeling and sorting of students into different and unequal educational pathways. *Tracking* (as this practice is known) relegated groups of students perceived as "higher status" to premium educational programs and others to much lower schooling. Historically, these groupings were based on criteria that most often resulted in segregating students by race and ethnicity.

Students placed in low tracks experienced dramatically reduced levels of educational attainment and left school with very limited life options. For this reason, tracking is recognized as a prime example of how separate is not equal; and for equity leaders, it is simply not acceptable. Tracking is an insidious past practice to which equity leaders now say, "Not on my watch!"

And yet this chapter is about what we call *new tracking*. This is a pervasive, unsound school design—a version of classic tracking—that goes dangerously unrecognized as one of the primary systemic inequity traps existing in schools and districts today. This chapter will demonstrate another way that "a rose by any other name" still has thorns!

## ONCE UPON A TIME, THERE WAS A PRINCIPAL

Mrs. May was the longtime principal of Smith Middle School. SMS was one of three middle schools located within the mostly middle-income area of the district. Mrs. May's voice carried a lot of weight across the district after her ten years as principal at SMS, as well as her ten years as a teacher in the same district prior to that. She was well-respected by her principal peers for her educational experience and deep relationships. She enjoyed the support of teachers and other staff for being a strong advocate for their interests.

As a teacher, she was a leader in the teachers' association, specializing in contract negotiations. Whenever a proposal for changes to the status quo came to the principal group, she would say, "Let's consider this from a teacher's perspective." Her responses were a not-so-veiled code saying, "I will not support anything that my teacher friends will complain to me about later." This had a great deal of influence on decisions at every level of the school system.

For most of its history, SMS served mostly students from White, middle-income families. When she began as principal of SMS ten years prior, developers began to build affordable housing across the way in the district, and the demographics of the schools in the district shifted. Latino, lower-income families rented the new apartments, and their children enrolled in most schools in the district. Housing development in the SMS attendance zone was the last phase of the city plan, so the demographics did not change at SMS until much later than they did at the rest of the schools.

As more Latino students enrolled at the other schools, the district worked to prepare schools to serve the needs of a more diverse student body. They provided administrators and staff with regular professional learning experiences on strategies for working with a wider range of student achievement levels. But Mrs. May only half listened.

She felt that most of that information was not relevant to her. She was proud that her school had stronger achievement than the other schools and believed that SMS was always the best school in the district. She did not connect the fact that SMS was the only one in the district where the community had remained the same over the longest period of time. Then, it happened.

## What Happened?

Five years later, apartment complexes sprung up in the SMS attendance zone. SMS student demographics shifted in what seemed like a flash. This made Mrs. May secretly nervous because she did not have experience working with students from different backgrounds. As the neighborhood changed, longtime families in her attendance zone saw "different" students enrolling.

The parents in these longtime families questioned whether their children could get the excellent education the school was known for "once those other students were in their school." They worried that teachers would have to teach down for the newer students, which would lower the caliber of education for their own children. Despite Mrs. May's reassurances, most families with financial resources moved to other neighboring cities where demographics had not changed.

Now SMS had 85% Latino and 15% White students, with 60% of students from lower-income families and 10% of students with disabilities. Mrs. May was responsible for students with whom she'd had no prior experience. Her equity knowledge level was low, and she had limited experience serving anyone other than White, middle-income students. As she reflected on her changing school conditions, Mrs. May felt a pang of threat that SMS could lose its long-standing status as the best school in the district. Mrs. May needed a way to maintain her best-school status. This was part of her identity and a source of her cache across the district.

She also wanted to help her newer students whose needs were a bit of a mystery to her. For the first time in her career, she felt ill-prepared as a leader.

## A Little Knowledge Is a Dangerous Thing

Mrs. May did not want to reveal her insecurities, so she drew upon the bits of information she'd gleaned from the district sessions she'd sort of attended over the years. What she did next is an example of a little knowledge being a dangerous thing! Motivated by the idea that diversity is an asset, Mrs. May decided that her equity leadership challenge was to keep the White students at her school. Yes, that is where she landed, and here was her logic.

Her thinking was that a mostly Latino school was bad because it would not have diversity. (Years later, she came to see the fallacies in her logic: her perception was that a mostly White student body was not a diversity problem, but a mostly non-White student body was inherently bad.) With her unique definition of diversity as the goal, she believed her task was to find a way to attract White—or just non-Latino—families.

Her approach was to design a program that would be attractive to those target students. Mrs. May had to respond to the parents' primary stated concern, which was the dumbing down of school to meet the needs of the new students. She needed to find a way to guarantee that the traditional neighborhood students would receive the excellent schooling SMS was known for in the community.

How could she make that guarantee? Could she create two separate programs, one for traditional neighborhood students and one for newer students? She had been around enough to know that *tracking* students was bad and not in step with current thinking on educational equity. She knew the following:

- Tracking was providing two distinct paths for students—different in many ways, one widely viewed as "not as good" as the other.
- Schools used to be blatant about separating students into *college tracks* and *vocational tracks*.

- The net effect of tracking was that students were assigned to a track by race, ethnicity, and family income.
- Assigned tracks determined the quality of students' educational experience, as well as their post-high school educational and life options.

So, her first impulse, a school-within-a-school plan was out. Mrs. May vowed that she would never, ever institute what she understood to be tracking. But a little knowledge is a dangerous thing, and the danger here is that Mrs. May didn't know what she didn't know. This is how it played out.

## WHERE DOES DIFFERENTIATION END AND TRACKING BEGIN?
She recalled professional readings discussing *differentiation* as a design to serve students with different needs. So she decided to structure her school for differentiation, a concept she saw as very different from tracking. Here was her thought process:

1. With tracking the quality of the education students receive differs significantly according to track.
   - So Mrs. May committed to providing *all students* with a high-quality education, regardless of their differing needs.
2. Tracking involves permanently keeping some students in a lower-quality program.
   - So she committed to allowing students to move from program to program based on specific, reasonable criteria (defined as achievement and work habits).

Grounded by those two personal pledges, Mrs. May proposed a draft of a differentiation plan to her leadership team of teachers, counselors, and the representatives of the parent groups she wanted to attract. Together they designed five differentiated options for students that evolved into the following list:

1. Advanced Academy—this was for students with either high academic achievement (test scores or grades) or strong work habits (based on teacher, principal, or parent recommendation).

2. Grade-level Academy—this was for students who qualified for the advanced academy by academic criteria but did not receive the work habits recommendation.

3. EL/Intervention A—this was for students considered beginning English learners. This generally started the year as a small group because they did not have many newcomers. So it became a good placement for students who enrolled during the school year, no matter their language proficiency.

4. EL/Intervention B—this was for students labeled intermediate and advanced English learners. They also used this as placement for native English speakers who struggled academically or had poor work habits. Some very vocal staff and parents advocated for having this option for students who just "were not making it" so they would not "hold the other classes back."

5. Special House—for students on individualized educational or 504 plans requiring accommodations or modifications. This option was also a placement for students suspected of having unidentified disabilities, especially involving behavior. Other classes endorsed not having these students disrupting their classes. This would be a win for the rest of school.

Mrs. May's perception was that establishing some safeguards would ensure that her new school design would not be tracking.

- She scheduled weekly classroom walk-throughs to personally ensure students received a high-quality program. Sometimes she invited leadership team members to walk with her so they could all have the same information in case they needed to make program refinements over time.

- To ensure that options did not become permanent placements, Mrs. May and the leadership team reviewed grades each semester and test scores at the end of every year. Any student who met one of these achievement criteria became a candidate for a higher option. Teachers received the list of candidates at the end of each year to weigh in on the work habits requirement. A thumbs-up from the teachers moved a student up, and a thumbs-down kept a student in their current option. Also, parents were invited to request level changes if they felt it best for their student.

While Mrs. May was committed to these tenets, her design evolved over the five years of this design, in the following ways:

- Materials—at first teachers used the same grade-level materials for each option. Fairly soon after, staff and Mrs. May made decisions about which materials best suited the needs of students at each option. Eventually, the advanced-option students received the grade-level curriculum, and the other options used more intervention-type (more gap-filling) curriculum.
- Student Placement Flexibility—next, the plan was to assign students to options by subject. For instance, a student could be in regular for language arts, but EL/Int A for mathematics. The same was theoretically true for the other core subjects. However, the staff saw that many students qualified for the same option in most, if not all, areas. So it became expedient to refer to students as "academy students," "regular students," "intervention kids," or "SpEds" and to place them in that respective option for every subject, based on those labels.
- Teacher Assignments—finally, when the design was instituted, Mrs. May assigned each teacher to classes from a variety of options. As the program evolved, teachers began to specialize in one option or another. This occurred for two major reasons—one public and one very private.

- The Public Reason—once each option began to use different materials for the same subject, teaching in different options meant multiple preps. Teachers expressed concern that teaching a class titled English 8 from three options meant they had to prepare for three different classes, not one. The contract between the district and the teachers' association restricted the number of preps per teacher, so the decision was made for teachers to be assigned to classes in only one option.

- The Private Reason—Mrs. May intended for every option to provide a high-quality education. However, in truth, some of her teachers were exceptional and some were less effective. Over time, parents from the advanced and regular options began to perceive the variability in teacher effectiveness, and actively campaigned for specific teacher assignments for their students' classes. Parents from other options were much less vocal. Mrs. May had ethical issues with making these changes, but dissatisfied parents strongly lobbied the district office and the board. In the end she acquiesced. She promised herself to work hard to improve the quality of instruction in the lower levels over time.

## Paris in the Springtime

Beginning the tenth year of Mrs. May's tenure as principal of SMS, the board hired a new superintendent. Dr. Paris was a highly experienced educator with twenty-twenty equity vision. Her entire disposition was to "go to work and look for trouble" (Avelar La Salle and Johnson 2018). That is, Dr. Paris committed to proactively identifying and shattering inequitable practices in her daily work. Her motivation was to ensure that every child would receive the premium education she knew they all deserved, but to which not all historically had access. As a systems thinker, she conducted a six-month learning tour of her new district, Pre-K to eighth grade.

After studying all the schools with a keen equity eye, Dr. Paris realized that SMS was a hot spot in serious need of attention. First, the superintendent quickly appreciated the influence that Mrs. May had across the district. This was not necessarily a terrible situation, except that conversations with Mrs. May made it clear that the design of SMS was severely misguided, and so Mrs. May's status could be a risk for the new superintendent.

In truth, the school was built for the needs of one community—the one Mrs. May was recruiting—at the expense of the others. In Dr. Paris's view, SMS was *tracking* students! It was a modern form of tracking, a "new tracking," shall we say. Nonetheless, it was tracking. This was a "not on my watch" (Avelar La Salle and Johnson 2018) situation for the new superintendent. She felt morally obligated to address it, regardless of the principal's influence across the district.

## A Short and Timely Retrospective

"Those who cannot remember the past are condemned to repeat it" is a quote originally attributed to a Spanish philosopher (Santayana 1905). We offer a brief review of the history of tracking in the United States to contextualize its current iteration and to guard against repeating it.

### *Tracking*

For over a century, tracking students was the way almost every school was designed. Readers may not realize that the practice or sorting and labeling students into permanent educational tracks began in American public schools in the 1850s. The practice was instituted in response to the influx of poor and unskilled immigrants from northern Europe and Asia.

Tracking was a way to follow compulsory school laws requiring all students to attend, while ensuring that "American" students were spared from interaction with less desirable students of color or certain immigrants. The explicit belief motivating tracking was that "less desirable" students were less intelligent than "real" American students and that they had poor hygiene, to boot (Salvatore et al. 2020)!

Tracking at the system level restricted students to segregated schools, with names such as Mexican schools, Colored schools, Chinese schools, and Indian boarding schools. Tracking within schools occurred by assigning students to different levels of classes, from high to low. The first measure used for making these sorting decisions came from an instrument thought to measure intelligence quotient (IQ). The results of the tests administered only in English confirmed the beliefs of many people of that time that entire groups of students were intellectually inferior.

Why raise a painful past now? We do so not to trigger feelings of guilt or victimization. We do so because our study of studies found that, even today, many school systems label and sort historically lower-achieving students in harmful ways. This occurs due to lack of equity knowledge expertise, misinformation, expediency, or even beliefs about differences in the intellectual capacity of different demographic student groups. Regardless of the reason, these forms of separating students into higher or lower quality educational pathways are just different enough from historical practices that they are not recognized as what they are: simply, new forms of tracking.

To some people, new tracking can appear just similar enough to differentiation that it seems like the right thing to do to meet student needs. However, over time, growing achievement gaps by demographic group confirm that new tracking is still tracking. Here is another example of the concept of $1^0\Delta$, as introduced in chapter 2.

## A Rose by Any Other Name Still Has Thorns

If you have a heavy equity heart reading about SMS, that is the appropriate reaction. "A rose by any other name is still a rose." And tracking by any other name is still tracking. As leader and chief program architect, Mrs. May was responsible for tracking students at her school. She did so unintentionally. Nonetheless, she created a new tracking program, a systemic inequity trap that snagged historically lower-achieving students.

Mrs. May is far from alone. A host of contemporary practices sort and label students in response to current, legitimate challenges, such as meeting the range of student needs. Yet the net effect is still systemically advantaging some student groups and disadvantaging others, most often by demographics. We issue a huge caution at this juncture. Many contemporary initiatives—as recent as those in response to the pandemic—are at high risk of becoming new tracking, as they already are labeling and sorting students in systemic ways.

Situate yourselves in the following scenario, and imagine that this occurred today. What would equity leaders think if legislators or other school system leaders required schools to

- accept only vulnerable students due to homelessness, foster care system involvement, having a disability, still learning English, or being low achieving; while
- all other students must be schooled virtually, on independent study, or some other form of learning away from campus?

How would the community of equity leaders respond? We sincerely hope that this would be rejected out of hand. Or, as we share in *Shattering Inequities* (2018), "Not on my watch!" Now consider the following what-ifs:

- *What if* the rationale for the proposal was to reduce on-campus student numbers to create very small group intervention classes for students who are far behind? Would that *what if* make the directives acceptable?
- *What if* the rationale was to reduce on-campus student numbers to create a nurturing setting to more easily incorporate social-emotional support for students experiencing trauma. Would that matter?
- *What if* the reason for following the directive was that, for the identified student groups, virtual schooling was as ineffective as no schooling, opening districts up to lawsuits? Would that be acceptable rationale?
- *What if* large sums of money were offered to districts who followed the directives as an incentive to do so? Would that be compelling?

Stop a moment and answer this question for yourself: Would any *what-if* make acceptable this systematic separation of students? If you, readers, lean toward saying yes, remember that *we know* that the criteria (students receiving special education services, students in foster care, etc.) *defaults in the separation* of students by racial, ethnic, and socioeconomic groups.

## Unsound Mandates

Our most sincere expectation is that equity champions everywhere would rise in protest against such a proposal to stigmatize students and relegate them to a less rigorous, more chaotic education, no matter how legitimate or compelling the rationale sounds. Yet school systems *did* implement unsound program designs much like, or exactly like, the one in the scenario. During pandemic school closures, most schools and districts followed mandates and financial incentives and simply rebranded hurtful sorting and labeling practices of the past.

We would be naïve to believe that people's limiting perceptions about historically lower-achieving students play no part in new tracking. Beliefs are often deep-seated feelings that people may not even recognize they carry. Once again, we are all mere mortals, subject to forming perceptions based on experiences and information unique to each person. However, rather than focusing on differential expectations, we focus here on overt, observable program design. Design can be objectively evaluated, adjusted, and corrected for immediate impact on students, whereas correcting harmful beliefs and expectations requires time our students do not have.

## New Tracking Litmus Test

What makes a practice new tracking despite the legitimate concerns motivating the design? Table 3.1 is Dr. Paris's five-point new tracking criteria that she applied to the SMS program to make that determination.

Dr. Paris's analysis indicated that SMS did, in fact, implement new tracking. Dr. Paris met with Mrs. May in her school office to discuss her impressions and concerns about the school design. Mrs. May vehemently rejected the notion that the program design at SMS advantaged some student groups and disadvantaged others. She felt sick at the suggestion that her school was sorting and labeling students. "What we do here is meet students where they are. And we have a wide range of needs at my school now," she rebutted.

Table 3.1 New Tracking Litmus Test

| Criteria | Smith Middle School | Is This "New Tracking"? | |
|---|---|---|---|
| | | No | Yes |
| 1. Curriculum and Materials<br><br>Are some student groups systematically excluded from grade-level core curriculum? | Only the advanced option gets grade-level core curriculum. The rest get different intervention programs with little connection to grade-level expectations. Even the grade-level group target standards that are a bit below grade level. | | Yes |
| 2. Placement Movement<br><br>Is there long-term exclusion from the premium program for some student groups? In this case, the premium program is the advanced path. | Only two students moved between levels over the past two years—one leveled up and one leveled down. The rest remained at the level they were initially placed.<br><br>Further, though English language arts criteria placement was used, all other subjects followed suit. | | Yes |

*(Continued)*

Table 3.1 Continued

| Criteria | Smith Middle School | Is This "New Tracking"? | |
|---|---|---|---|
| | | No | Yes |
| 3. Student Placement Profile<br><br>Has the practice resulted in racial/ethnic or other segregation? | The advanced group are 20% of the students at school but are disproportionately representative of the student body at large:<br><br>• 80% of all White students are in advanced<br>• 20% of all Latino students are in advanced<br><br>All other program options involve 80% of school students:<br><br>• 80% of all Latino students are placed here<br>• 20% of all White students are here<br><br>Also, a group of Latino students who tested grade level on previous state exams were not assigned to the advanced and, sometimes, not even the regular options. Conversely, a group of White students who were not on grade level on previous measures were assigned to the advanced option. The stated reasons were either expectations on the counselors' part, a teacher rating of work habits, or parent insistence. | | Yes |
| 4. Student Academic Success<br><br>Are students who are placed in the lower paths disproportionately experiencing academic failure? | The average grades for advanced-option students were:<br><br>• 75% A or B grades<br>• 15% C grades<br>• 10% D or F grades<br><br>The average grades for all-other-option students were:<br><br>• 23% A or B grades<br>• 12% C grades<br>• 65% D or F grades | | Yes |

5. Student Perception

Are students in lower paths stigmatized for their assignment to a specific path?

Here are representative language samples from different roles:

Principal—the options attract target families. They also provide specific support for students who always struggle. Eventually, struggling students will move up to grade level.

Counselors—our model makes student placement easy. By now, we know who goes where even without reviewing the placement data.

Teachers from Advanced Option—for once, we can be fair to students who we know will be going to college after graduation.

Teachers from Other Options—the most important thing for our students is that we help them regain their self-esteem. We know how hard their lives are so we intentionally provide them with a program where they can be successful.

Students from All Options—everyone knows which classes are for the smarter kids.

Parents of Advanced Option Students—my kids are at this school because they are in the best classes with kids like them.

Parents of Other Option Students—I trust the principal and the teachers. I support whatever they think is best for my child.

Yes

Note: Dr. Paris found differences of opinion from each group she interviewed. However, the statements listed here represent the prominent theme expressed by each group.

CHAPTER 3

## How Could I?

The superintendent walked Mrs. May through a deep review of her school data by overlapping demographics, program placement, and student outcomes. The reports went back five years. Also, Dr. Paris kindly but factually shared her insights about SMS from observations and interviews she did over the first semester.

She then did a step-by-step think aloud, connecting what she'd observed to the student achievement profile for those previous five years of Mrs. May's principalship at SMS. She pointed out the obvious difference in results by demographics and the fact that the gap between White students and Latino students grew over that period. White students were generally at grade level or above, while most Latino students were falling further and further behind grade level. We will spare readers the details of the entire conversation. Just know that after ninety minutes, Mrs. May was inconsolable.

"How could I do this to my students? My families? My community?" She, like so many leaders, gave it her best attempt, but she did not have the necessary equity knowledge level and experience to design an appropriate response to her changing demographics. Neither the district nor anyone else had been there to guide her. So to arrive at her response, she'd combined small bits of equity understanding with community pressure and probably some different unstated expectations for student groups.

The final part of the office conversation was Dr. Paris reviewing some final data bites with the principal.

- As a rule, White students in the advanced option qualified because of the work habits criterion, not necessarily for being on grade level. This defaulted into the disproportionate placement of White students into this option because these students were perceived to be the most serious students.
  - Though many students in this option were not academically strong when initially placed, the longer they were in the advanced option, the stronger their achievement level became.
  - By eighth grade, they performed at the highest achievement level in the school on every measure.

- In contrast, a group of Latino students with a long history of academic proficiency were assigned to the regular option or lower, also on the work habit criterion.
  - Though this group of students were academically strong when placed, the longer they remained in that option, the lower their achievement became on every measure. This was also true for the other students placed here.

"What is your takeaway from the data and our time together today?" asked the superintendent. In a rare, vulnerable moment, Mrs. May shared that she was crushed by the realization that her school hurt students. "I feel guilty, broken, and overwhelmed," she said. Dr. Paris simplified the design problem into the two equity principles to clarify where Mrs. May went wrong.

1. *Equity leaders make all decisions anchored on a commitment to provide every student with a premium education.* The current design ignored this principle in that different options resulted in very different educational rigor and quality, only one of which was acceptable for any student.

2. *Decisions that impact the educational experiences we provide students must be grounded by this fundamental goal of getting to X; that is, where we can no longer predict student outcomes by demographics.* The design at SMS sorted and labeled students in a way that defaulted into separating students by race and ethnicity. Consequently, the gap between the White and Latino students grew throughout the years that the options design was in place.

The superintendent explained that the unintended consequence of violating these two principles was the institutionalization of new tracking, a systemic inequity trap that created insurmountable barriers for students assigned to all but the highest option.

## Dr. Paris's Grace and Equity Leadership

Dr. Paris helped Mrs. May understand the interplay between her school design, her own implicit beliefs and expectations, and her student outcomes over the decade she was principal. After a deep, reflective pause, Mrs. May admitted that she was now clear about where she went wrong.

She also recognized that she just did not have the energy, spirit, knowledge, or confidence to lead the required changes in the school direction. She was of retirement age and felt like the school would be best served by a different leader, one with the equity knowledge level she lacked. The next morning, Mrs. May personally submitted her letter of intent to retire at the end of the school year. Dr. Paris read the letter, honored Mrs. May's decades of service, and accepted the resignation.

Mrs. May ended her career with her head held high and bags packed for a move back to her native Hawaii for a well-deserved new chapter in her life.

### IS THERE A *TRUE, RIGHT, AND JUST* ALTERNATIVE TO NEW TRACKING?

Yes, there is! Here are the practical guidelines that Dr. Paris presented to the new principal. The most basic principle requires us to remember the law of straight lines from our geometry class, which was, for most of us, a long time ago! Stated simply (oversimply, for our math expert friends),

- The shortest distance between two points is a straight line.

Dr. Paris made the case for the equity leader's law of a straight line, as depicted in figure 3.1.

Read the graphic in the following way. At the left end is a student's current academic level. At the other end is the goal—grade-level achievement or above. There is distance between those two points, showing that the student is not at grade level.

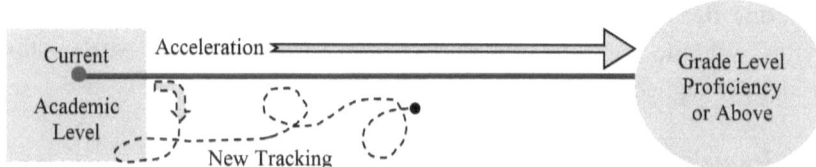

**Figure 3.1** The Equity Leader's Law of a Straight Line

- *Acceleration* approaches are represented by the direct arrow between the students' current academic level and grade-level expectations.
  - These approaches directly support grade-level expected outcomes for all students.
  - Any gaps in student learning are addressed as they arise.
  - But student instruction is always in the expected grade-level curriculum.
- *New tracking* approaches are represented by the curvy line between current achievement levels and grade level.
  - These approaches remediate academic deficiencies prior to presenting students with access to grade-level curriculum. Since these approaches fill gaps from previous grade levels, the direction of instruction is sometimes moving away from grade level, sometimes delving deeper into a concept, or covering something not directly in grade-level expected outcomes. Therefore, the curvy line moves in various directions. Students in these programs almost never reach grade level, which is why the curvy line stops well before the grade-level goal.
  - Sometimes student deficit areas are diagnosed and then addressed.
  - Other times, specific deficits are not diagnosed, but students who are not on grade level are assigned to a remedial curriculum that teachers use as an alternative to the grade-level material.
  - Finally, students may be assigned to the remedial curriculum as a supplement to the grade-level program. In any event, the goal is to prepare students with foundational skills as a prerequisite to expecting students to be successful during grade-level instruction.

The superintendent clarified the characteristics of each approach intended to help struggling students. Table 3.2 compares both approaches. What do you notice as you review the comparison table?

**Table 3.2** Comparison of New Tracking and Acceleration

| New Tracking | Acceleration |
| --- | --- |
| Slow down, simplify instructional goals<br>• Meeting students where they are<br>• Slow group inference | Goal is on-time learning with peers<br>• All students in grade-level core<br>• Students in core heterogeneous classes |
| Learning loss, unfinished learning, intervention<br>• Diagnose "gaps"<br>• Place students by level for large periods of time in a day, year, or over years<br>• Teach missing skills before moving to grade level | Accelerated learning taught within core lessons<br>• Frequent checks for understanding of core<br>• Small group and individual-guided practice of core and core prerequisite skills led by teacher<br>• Varied ways to present a concept using multiple modalities and approaches |
| Assessments from programs<br>• Focus is testing skills in isolation, not on grade-level content<br>• Assessments measure program goals, not grade-level core | Frequent progress monitoring on grade-level content<br>• Focus is frequent feedback on teaching-learning success of core<br>• Teaching adjustments respond to feedback right away |
| Values materials/software implementation<br>• May not even involve a live teacher or other professional | Student engagement is viewed as a learning accelerant<br>• Interesting, emotionally supportive, regular cognitive and physical state changes, and values class relationships |
| Passive and boring<br>• Often worksheets, packets, software, or repetitive drills | Active and fun<br>• Relevant, social, supportive, energizing, inspiring, and enjoyable |
| A mash-up of well-meaning efforts<br>• Activity but not accomplishment | There is one coherent design<br>• Structured tiers of support for the core, delivered daily—during the regular school day and extended beyond |
| Decelerates learning<br>• Student achievement levels get further away from grade level | Accelerates learning<br>• Student achievement grows more than one year's worth of learning for one year of school |

When the new principal reviewed the comparison table, she said something that made Dr. Paris know she had selected the right principal. "Everyone is implementing remedial programs and gap-filling tutoring. Sometimes they call it differentiation or interventions. Often, these are really just new forms of tracking!"

*The Acceleration Formula*
How do we teach at grade level to students who are behind and have them learn more than one grade level in a school year? What does an acceleration program look like in practice? Is there an acceleration formula? Absolutely! The next step for Dr. Paris was to help the new principal create a school design for SMS based on that very formula.

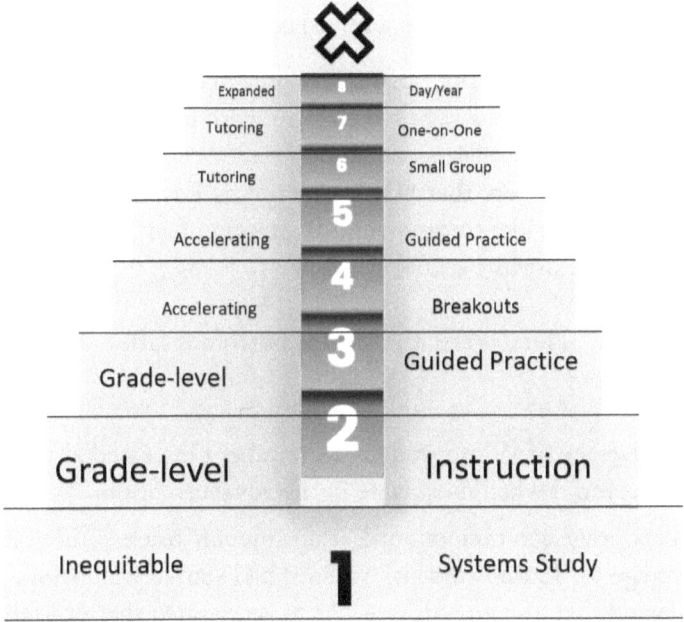

**Figure 3.2** The Acceleration Formula

First, the superintendent and new principal agreed on a single grade-level program—no optional levels. Then, to plan for getting all students to successfully learn at grade level, Dr. Paris showed the principal figure 3.2, which is a version of a familiar model of tiered support for individual students. However, this model is adapted for systemwide acceleration of learning for lower-achieving students. This adaptation departs from the familiar tiered model in three important ways:

1. This model presumes the law of straight lines (figure 3.1). That is, every student starts at the first rung, with grade-level instruction. *Every support level* after that is a preview or review of grade-level-expected learning, taught in a manner that best fits the needs of specific students (i.e., using manipulatives for math, physical gestures for learning vocabulary, or listening to text on tape prior to reading it in class). At no time are students assigned to programs or curriculum not directly aimed at expectations of grade level.

2. The second difference is that, unlike the familiar three-tiered model, this version has up to eight opportunities for students to reach at least proficiency on grade-level expectations.

3. Finally, in this version, students are provided all these support levels they require *in one day*. Students begin with layer 2 during core class time, and all the subsequent support tiers are built into the structure of each day. (Note that first instruction is Layer 2. This is because Layer 1 is the identification and shattering of any systemic inequity traps that exist in a school system.)

Did it work? Here were the SMS outcomes after five years of implementation:

- The average of White student achievement increased at the same rate as it did when most were in the advanced option.
- The average achievement of Latino students reached the state average for Latino students, when it had started well below. Beyond that, the growth rate was so accelerated that projections

were that Latino students were on target to meet the average achievement for higher-income students in the state.

- During this period the school earned a host of accolades and awards for high achievement with Latino and lower-income students. They earned the federal Title I Blue Ribbon Award, the national award for highest growth for that student group, and the Business Roundtable Award for the greatest increase in math achievement for what they called "nontraditional" students.

- The demographics remained at 85 percent Latino and 15 percent White during this period. The new design and highly publicized academic successes had no impact on changing the student population. Parents who moved to other districts chose to remain there for a variety of reasons. It became clear that some parents simply preferred that their children not be schooled with the newer students.

The most exciting outgrowth of the SMS story is that their success inspired the four neighboring districts to abandon their new tracking programs and adopt the acceleration formula. These districts sustained this effort for over a decade, when a large organization picked up the story. They focused on the community impact of the seventeen-year coordinated efforts of the local school districts. They emphasized that during that time, the racial and ethnic profile of the community remained unchanged. The following is an excerpt from that article that describes how life for residents changed over time as the average level of educational attainment increased.

> *The share of residents with less than a high school diploma fell from 30% in 2000 to 10% in 2017, while the college graduation rate grew by 15 percentage points. These educational gains, in turn, improved community livelihoods. In 2016, only 12% of households had incomes below the federal poverty line, well below the county average, where the figure had been 30%. Moreover, median income increased for every neighborhood in the districts from 2000 to 2016, with the*

*aggregated average growing from $40,463 to $68,451 in 2016, well above the county neighborhood average of $55,000.*

So did the acceleration formula work? You decide!

## Summary

In this chapter we meet Mrs. May, a principal with a sincere desire to serve her students and community. She and her leadership team created a set of programs designed to meet the range of student needs at her school. She also hoped that the design would help her maintain what she understood to be diversity in student demographics that she valued. What she came to understand was that her design created a system for labeling and sorting students into programs that were not equivalent in quality. Worse, the practice defaulted into grouping students by demographics. This resulted in systematically advantaging one group of students and disadvantaging the rest. Unintentionally, the school instituted a modern form of tracking—new tracking. This chapter is a flashing yellow light to equity leaders to be vigilant and ensure that the current goal of meeting student needs does not devolve into a new version of old tracking practices—After all, a rose by any other name still has thorns!

## Equity Concepts

- Tracking—the harmful historic practice of sorting and labeling historically lower-achieving students that segregates them and relegates them to a lesser quality education.

- New Tracking—the current practice of sorting and labeling students with the intent of meeting their needs but that, ultimately, has the same detrimental effects as previous forms of tracking.

- Acceleration Formula—an alternative to new tracking that is a systems model of ensuring that lower-achieving students have access to and a rich opportunity to meet grade-level expectations with the support needed to reach grade-level proficiency in a not-too-far time in the future.

**ACTIONABLE TOOLS**

Now is the time for you, readers, to check for new tracking in your own school or district. We invite you and a team to use the online templates to more deeply consider the implications of new tracking in your school system. Locate the fillable templates at https://orendaed.org/WhereEquityLives/.

## Chapter 4

# The Christmas Tree Effect

*Equity Hook: The Thing of the Thing*

Have you ever wondered

- whether a program exists anywhere in the world that will be the solution to your worry over the historical lower achievement of the same student groups, over and over;
- why the people you lead do not always share your enthusiasm for new and exciting initiatives to help struggling students; or
- how it is that the more solutions you bring to help historically lower-performing students, the less they seem to impact students?

These questions can be answered by the next one of the five most common systemic inequity traps identified through our study of studies—the Christmas Tree Effect. The equity hook for this chapter, "The Thing of the Thing," is the memory trigger for this concept, the meaning of which will become clear as you meet the protagonist of this chapter, Derek Hart.

Derek Hart, a high school principal, was an equity champion from the time he was a young science teacher in an inner-city middle school, serving primarily African American, lower-income students. He identified with his students in many ways and was certain that they were capable of much higher levels of academic success. He remembered feeling underestimated as a student all through school, especially in math and science. These feelings motived him to become a science teacher.

As a teacher, Derek was troubled by a few things. First, he was a very energetic, effective teacher even during his first year. Teaching was his passion, and he planned to be a positive force in every way possible at his school. However, he felt disheartened that so many of his colleagues seemed so jaded. They just signed in and out of school each day with little enthusiasm for their profession or their students. It was draining on him as a new, young, excited teacher.

He once discreetly asked a few teachers why they always seemed so grumpy. They told him they were once idealistic like Derek. They recounted different ways they were not supported over the years, even with their most urgent issues. These included things like the need to assess students with learning difficulties, getting help for a family in crisis, wanting to learn strategies for meeting the needs of the wide range of student achievement in their classes, or even just wanting their projector bulb changed (remember those?).

Teachers were even more aggravated at the seemingly endless list of school and district priorities that came out of nowhere and changed every year. They felt overwhelmed and generally off-kilter all the time. They said they slowly started caring less and less after days, months, and years of not feeling like successful teachers. Derek could not believe they would admit that. He was personally aghast at their lack of commitment as educators though he was too respectful to say anything to them.

Over time he developed relationships with his colleagues. He began to understand them more and dislike them less. People talk about teacher burn out. But Derek realized that his colleagues had not burned out. Instead, they had fizzled out. It was more of a slow smothering of their dedication, which was replaced by confusion and then frustration; helplessness; hostility; and, finally, apathy. It was like the stages of grief over the loss of professional passion.

## Activity Does Not Equal Accomplishment

Derek thought it was ironic that teachers, counselors, and other staff did not feel supported. The district was known for being on the cutting edge of trends in education. If a new idea appeared on the education scene, their district immediately brought it to the schools. During his seven years as a teacher, he remembered attending sessions about mastery learning, standards-based grading, formative assessment, parent involvement, active engagement strategies, technology in the classroom, English language development, schoolwide discipline plan, personalized learning, multitiered systems of support (MTSS), trauma-informed practices, mindfulness, professional learning communities, understanding data, culturally relevant schools, and safe schools. There were more, but they were a blur.

Even *his* equity muscle weakened during those years. Teachers were frequently pulled out of class for this or that training. Not all teachers went, though. Derek was not sure how that was decided, but he was out all the time, while many other teachers stayed back. Some days were just nuts. Between the substitute teachers needed to release teachers for training and those required to cover for absent teachers, students went multiple days without their regular teachers.

Site administrators were also frequently pulled off campus for a variety of meetings intended to improve and accelerate student outcomes, though their topics were very different from what the teachers received. Sometimes all of this occurred on the same days. Returning to school the next day was truly crazy! The students' understanding was that not much learning was expected when so many people were out.

The counselors, who rarely left campus for district meetings, complained about having to pick up the slack when teachers and administrators were off campus. Whenever the principal and assistant principals were not at school, counselors were responsible for answering questions from substitutes, problem solving for students, handling discipline, responding to parents, addressing facility problems, and handling any other unexpected issues that regularly arose. They begrudgingly joked among themselves that this must constitute the part of their job description titled "other duties as assigned." Derek noticed that the days after teachers and administrators were out, many counselors were absent. Everyone just figured that they needed time to recover from the looniness of the previous days.

CHAPTER 4

The irony was that no matter how much the school and district tried, outcomes for historically lower-achieving students did not improve. Plus, adults on campus grew grouchier! Derek intuitively understood that something was fundamentally wrong with this picture. The district hired people who were excited about providing a premium education to every student.

But soon the conditions all but extinguished that true, right, and just spark. What were those conditions? Well, they had to do with Christmas trees!

### *The Christmas Tree Effect*

Bryk (1993) writes about "Christmas Tree Schools," a characterization that befits Derek's school. This refers to schools that expend human and financial resources on too many simultaneous initiatives. Like ornaments on a tree, each effort sparkles and attracts lots of attention. However, just as overly decorating a tree takes away from its beauty, so too does piling on one initiative atop the next take away the impact on accelerating achievement. Simply stated, when it comes to efforts to shatter systemic inequities in schools and districts, more is not necessarily better (Johnson and Avelar La Salle 2010).

The bottom line is that taking on too many efforts results in the Christmas Tree Effect, no matter how "research-based" or how much a plan represents "best practices." And then getting to *X marks the spot* is almost assuredly a distant dream.

## HART BREAK

Derek's school became a casualty of the Christmas Tree Effect. Sadly, over time, even Derek became cynical and critical of the whirlwind flurry of priorities and programs at his school and district. However, unlike many of his other colleagues, his equity heart never allowed him to become complacent. Instead, he resolved to one day become a decision maker in the district so he could make the changes he thought students deserved. With that impetus, five years later, Derek became the principal of a neighboring school, True High School (THS).

True High was in a lower-income part of the district, where student outcomes were traditionally low but notably lower for African American students than for others. On his first tour of the school, he was pleased that the campus seemed orderly and calm. Derek loved being at the high school and saw students around campus having fun with friends and generally being the typical teens he enjoyed so much. This principalship gave Derek the fresh start he needed to recharge his enthusiasm for his mission to educate all students at the highest level.

However, he was dismayed at what he saw on his first classroom visits. Those same students who were so joyful out on campus were almost completely detached from class instruction. Most were not disruptive, just ultrapassive and obviously bored. Many students fidgeted with their phones. Others passed notes. And still others just sat there, staring at the walls.

Derek assumed all classes ran like the high-energy, challenging classes he delivered as a science teacher. That was not the case at all. Even Derek struggled to remain attentive during his class visits, and he was the principal! Several teachers chatted with him when he walked into their classroom and pointed out the lack of student interest. They attributed it to the inability of students to keep up.

But Derek's observation was that teachers oversimplified the content to well below grade level, making classes extremely basic—and boring. Typical instruction consisted of some lecture and then the assignment of an independent book or website activity. Honestly, teachers appeared as bored as the students. Where was all the training the district had provided over the years?

Derek noted something else. He felt an undertone of antagonism when he entered classrooms. Signs were not overt, but teachers certainly did not welcome him with a bright smile and open arms. Once again, he found himself at a school where it seemed he was the only one excited about providing their students with the exceptional education regularly afforded students in other parts of the district. This was his chance to make a real difference. Not knowing exactly how to proceed, Derek phoned a friend.

CHAPTER 4

## Hart and Soul

Alma was a trusted friend from another district. Derek and Alma had been in the same administrative credentialing program cohort for three years. They had the same urgency to close historic student achievement gaps, so they teamed up on many projects during the program. In fact, they worked together so often that their cohort mates teasingly called them Hart and Soul (*Alma* means soul in several languages: Derek Hart was his name. Get it?).

Since completing their program, Derek and Alma had become professional sounding boards for one another. It was Derek's turn to call upon his dear friend for thought partnership. In the first conversation with Alma, Derek shared his initial impressions:

- lackluster teaching and learning
- oversimplified expectations for students
- an undercurrent of apathy about getting to $X$
- overall adult and student disengagement with school
- emotional distance between staff and students
- overall low achievement but a large gap between students representing different demographics

Derek made a painful admission. He was beginning to question his ability to lead his school. He feared that the culture of apathy and negativity could rub off on him. He was already tiptoeing around feelings of defeat. Alma visited the campus, walked through classes, met students, and chatted with staff. After a full day, she'd collected a long list of gripes shared with her.

After school Alma met Derek at a local coffee shop to discuss the list. Derek saw the pages of writing and became visibly emotional. Heartfelt leader that he was (all puns fully intended!), he took a deep breath and asked to see the notes. He was mustering up the strength to tackle each item, one at a time. As he reached over to grab the notes from Alma, she pulled the pages away. Derek braced himself for her next move. He trusted in her wisdom and perspective.

## A Soul-Full Conversation

>Alma: I see that you are experiencing lots of emotions, Derek.
>
>Derek: Yes, I am. I just want to hurry up and fix the things you found so we can move on to all the ideas I have for making this school an amazing place for students and staff.
>
>Alma: Of course you do. You are tired of pushing people to do the right thing for kids who need a fair shot at a good life. You hate that everyone does not seem to share your belief in the capability of all students to reach the highest academic levels. Here is a question for you: What could create a vibrant school culture that would result in giving every student a premium education?
>
>Derek: Well, right now, I'm angry at everyone for treating their positions like a job where you just clock in and out. They must need more information, training, or I don't know what! I know that the school has provided many, many professional learning opportunities over the years. On top of that, the previous principal administered a survey where staff listed topics of interest, and the school provided at least one session on each request, and there are over seventy staff members! Staff meeting agendas listed topics like block scheduling, standards-based grading, overviews of materials they purchased, using technology in the classroom, mindfulness, classroom management, parent engagement, and more. I don't understand what is happening here, but it cannot be a lack of support.

We are certain that many equity leaders feel for Derek's situation, based on either personal experience or sheer empathy. Our certainty is backed by a 2018 Gallop poll that reveals the following:

- Defined by enthusiasm and commitment for their work and their school, about 30 percent of teachers are fully engaged, while 70 percent of teachers are either "not engaged" or "actively disengaged." This mirrors engagement of employees in most sectors.

- About 50 percent of students are engaged, while the other half of students are either "not engaged" or "actively disengaged" in their schooling.
  - Engaged students are 2.5 times more likely to report having excellent grades and doing well in school.
  - Engaged students are 4.5 times more likely to feel hopeful about their future (Hodges 2018).

## How Much Is Too Much?

Part of Derek's discussion with Alma was around this question: Could the problem be as simple as having too much "support"? That is, are there just too many priorities at once? Is there a right number of projects that school and district staff can handle? There is *almost* a right answer to that question. Researchers are certain that the human brain has a limit to how much it can actively process at one time.

But there exists no specific agreement about the precise amount of novel information people can actively process. Findings of empirical studies in this area estimate that answer to be somewhere between three (Gilchrist, Cowan, and Naveh-Benjamin 2008) and seven (Miller 1956) chunks, depending on how a chunk of information is defined.

School systems seeking to get to $X$ are at the greatest risk of expecting leaders and staffs to implement much more than what is humanly or systemically possible to do well. As career-long advocates for historically lower-achieving student groups, we offer the following practical guidelines. School systems can

- deeply attend to *one* focus area;
- engage in some way with *two* focus areas;
- feign attention to at least parts of *three* focus areas; or
- not even pretend to be engaged in *four* or more areas of focus.

Compare the guidelines to the number of programs, initiatives, practices, campaigns, and efforts in your school system. Is there any connection between that number of efforts and the strength or weakness of your school system's track record of accelerating student achievement?

## When You're Lost, Stop and Ask for Directions

It became clear to Derek that at least part of the trouble at his school was that they had too many things going on at once. That awareness helped him dial down his emotional meter, and his objectivity returned. Now Derek wanted to openly and honestly go directly to the staff with his observations and reflections. No matter the outcome, Derek felt that the discussion would inform his next steps and help the school move toward X. Derek was reinvigorated as an equity leader, or, as he put it, "I finally feel unstuck!"

So, leading with his equity foot forward, he decided to share his observations and reflections at the next staff meeting. Alma suggested that it would be prudent to share his thoughts with the entire staff at once so everyone could hear the same message. Alma shared that an open forum with the entire group could become unproductive. Derek and Alma designed a discussion protocol to help guide trusted staff and administrators to serve as facilitators during the table talks after his presentation. The following section includes the discussion protocol and summarizes the major themes across all the table groups.

## Discussion Summary

*"Do you believe students are invested in school and their academic future? Explain."*

The response was that the most common theme was that most students were disengaged. They were compliant but not excited about learning, and they had no school spirit. The exceptions were students in the higher-level classes. These tended to be students from historically higher-achieving groups with a long history of academic success prior to high school. One table asked why the demographics of the higher-level classes were different from those in lower-level classes?

*"Do you believe the staff is personally invested in the school and its mission to provide every student with a premium education? Explain."*

## Chapter 4

Three ideas emerged. First, the staff was shocked at Principal Derek's observation that they were not very engaged in school or with students. They expressed a range of emotions. The second was the admission that individuals only know what they feel and do, so Derek's observations could be true "for others." Finally, the staff strongly agreed that the school had too many things that the staff was responsible for implementing. Again, the staff expressed the entire gamut of emotions during this part of the discussion.

*"What suggestions do you have to address these issues?"*

The conversation was almost the same at every table. Here are some quotes: "The district expects too much." "The school is all over the place." "Everyone is doing their own thing." "It is impossible to do everything well." "I get evaluated by people who don't understand the challenges of doing my job." "We wish we could be better at our jobs, our students deserve it." "Nothing that is mandated is effective with our students." "We are doing the best we can, but we just can't keep up with all the demands." "Whatever the topic of the day is, this, too, shall pass if we just wait it out."

One quote stood out because it came from one of the most positive, reflective, and student-connected staff members. She shared that even her passion for her profession was strained. She was committed to doing an excellent job for her students, but with so many different things constantly coming at her, she just wanted to understand, What is the priority? What really matters? *What is the thing of the thing!*

She said that, years ago, the district had a clear focus on closing student achievement gaps and that the school had one strategy—alignment. She resisted at first because it was new and she didn't understand the point. But they kept that focus for four of the best years she ever had as a teacher. The initiative was smart, doable, and students responded positively. But little by little, they got different principals, different district administrators, and each had some signature piece they added. Now the original alignment focus is unrecognizable though some vestiges remained.

She had an emotional request. She wished staff would be supported and held accountable for implementing one priority that would not change . . . for a decade, at least. From experience she felt that amount of time was necessary to learn something well enough to implement it in a way that has a real impact on the students who need the most help.

"*What is the thing of the thing?*" This resonated with Derek very strongly.

"*What else should we consider that hasn't come up yet?*"

No one responded to this question at their table group. However, a small group of staff members asked to meet with Derek in his office. The delegation shared that they did not agree with most of the staff. The district did not demand too much. The school and district initiatives were opportunities to grow as equity champions and educators. They saw a clear connection between all the programs the school was involved in over the years. Everything made perfect sense to them, and they'd found ways to incorporate all those new skills into their practice. They said, "We don't know why they complain so much." This, too, resonated with Derek.

As a follow-up to the staff meeting, Derek created a small focus team of his three administrators, two department heads, the head of counseling, a district administrator, two students, a parent who also worked as an attendance clerk at the school, and Alma. They spent a week reviewing the data that showed their overall depressed student achievement and the achievement gaps by demographic group. This pattern had remained constant for over a decade.

The team's charge was to understand why student achievement did not improve despite so many school and district attempts. They opened up and talked about the school culture of disengagement with the mission to get to $X$—the condition Derek spent so much time trying to understand. They even got comfortable enough to admit that not every adult on campus believed in the capability of all students to succeed at high academic levels. (A hard truth is that hurtful beliefs and expectations related to historically lower-achieving students are always at the root of systemic inequity traps.)

CHAPTER 4

## IT'S *WHAT* YOU KNOW

Over the week the action team was honest and receptive. They arrived at one major epiphany. The team admitted that underneath the Christmas Tree Effect was the most difficult issue to discuss openly. It was their observation that not all equity champions are equipped to make decisions about what to prioritize to get historically lower-achieving students to $X$.

Having an equity heart for students is necessary, but it is not sufficient. Equity leaders must develop a threshold of expertise on what school systems can do to help get students *to X*. From the experience of many team members, the district and school leaders lacked that expertise. Derek agreed and gently suggested that the expertise was also limited at True HS.

It is simple to tell school and district leaders to just stop adding initiatives. It is easy to blame the bad attitudes of adults as the reason for limited student growth. However, the program shopping and negativity are only symptoms of something deeper. In the next section, we introduce a deeper condition that manifests in the Christmas Tree Effect and the related culture of apathy—the difference in equity leadership expertise.

### *The Novice-Expert Continuum*

There exists a rich academic literature base that describes key differences between novices and experts that are extremely relevant to this discussion (Schunn and Patchan 2009). As Derek experienced and our study of studies demonstrates, having the title of a leader does not necessarily come with the expertise required to get students to $X$ *marks the spot*. It also explains why many staff members felt overwhelmed by all the programs at their school, while for some, the efforts made perfect sense.

Have you ever watched a movie with someone who interpreted it completely differently from you, almost like you watched different movies? In the same way, novices and experts can be part of the same experience yet perceive it completely differently. It is as if people with different levels of expertise actually "see" differently. Table 4.1 lists some of the differences between the novices and experts, with leadership examples for each. As you review the table, do any of the descriptions resonate with your experience?

**Table 4.1** Differences between Novices and Experts

| Novices | Experts |
|---|---|
| **Focus on superficial aspects of new learning** | **Easily identify the underlying principles of new information and know how to apply or adapt them** |
| *Leaders learn that tracking is bad, so they make sure to group students heterogeneously in core classes. But they do not object to the lower-performing students being grouped at one table, resulting in a remedial group within the classes.* | *Leaders understand the history of tracking, so they ensure that all classes are heterogeneous. Leaders help teachers learn to frequently check for understanding and provide small group support to struggling students as part of the class.* |
| Leaders often overgeneralize concepts from one context to another because situations appear similar on the surface | Leaders distinguish between concepts that should and should not be generalized |
| *Leaders learn that English learners need instruction in language development, so they require schools to provide a period of English language development (ELD) for every English learner, which denies them the opportunity to access the full premium program.* | *Leaders know that English learners who have been in English-speaking schools for over four years and newcomers require different support. Schools are directed to provide the extra ELD period for newcomers. But long-term English learners are in all premium classes placed heterogeneously, with teachers who incorporate language development into lessons as needed.* |
| Leaders become easily overwhelmed by new information because every new learning seems like a new point in a list of unique content | Leaders do not become easily overwhelmed by new information because they can see connections between new ideas and what they already know |
| *Leaders become comfortable participating in the nested data system but become flustered when asked to facilitate data reflection sessions because they see that as something completely different.* | *Leaders learn to facilitate data reflection sessions with their teacher teams and quickly feel comfortable doing the same for guidance teams. Though the data and process are somewhat different, leaders see clear parallels in the two processes.* |

| | |
|---|---|
| Leaders often think they know more than they do about equity concepts | Leaders often consult with other equity experts to check their thinking |
| *Leaders approve the purchase of any materials that proport to support struggling students.* | *Leaders understand the capacity limit of their school or district—and of themselves—to support and monitor quality program implementation. They adopt a very small number of initiatives and defer the rest.* |

**Table 4.2** Continuum of Equity Leadership Expertise

| Levels of Expertise | This Level Is Able to . . . | Understanding of Equity Leadership Issues Includes . . . | Common Descriptors |
|---|---|---|---|
| Level 1<br><br>*Novice* | • Remember facts<br>• Follow steps and procedures | Basic concepts of educational fairness | Conscientious<br>Literal<br>Unsure<br>Emotional |
| Level 2 | • Apply background knowledge to familiar situations | Enough *background* to question whether practices work against *getting to X* | Eager<br>Rehearsed<br>Overconfident |
| Level 3 | • Apply background knowledge to unfamiliar situations<br>• Research answers for unfamiliar problems | Enough *background and experience* to see systemic inequity traps not obvious to others and to understand how beliefs and expectations relate to those practices | Competent<br>Independent<br>Resourceful<br>Confident<br>Effective |
| Level 4<br><br>*Expert* | • Arrive at effective solutions to novel situations by<br>  • applying complex reasoning<br>  • integrating information from various sources<br>  • making connections others cannot see | Enough *background, experience,* and *intuition* to see systemic inequity traps unique to a context, understand motivating beliefs and expectations, and design a tailored solution to fit that specific situation | Strategic<br>Intuitive<br>Trusted<br>Mature<br>Gracious<br>Collaborative<br>Self-confident |

For Derek, differences in expertise explained a great deal about the varied reactions he observed in colleagues when he was a teacher and now as principal. It also explained why there was so much program shopping.

## THE THING OF THE THING

Underdeveloped equity leadership expertise in schools and districts results in leadership decisions that send human and financial resources *every which way*. Districts and schools often become a motley mix of programs, initiatives, conferences, consultants, and materials. It is the "Let's throw everything at the wall and see what sticks" response. Often, novices become program shoppers searching in vain for the silver bullet. The antidote to this is to develop a critical mass of decision makers across a school system who have an "expert" level of equity leadership knowledge and expertise.

This is precisely what Derek's action team discovered was the greatest need at their school. Their most important focus, what they called the *thing of the thing*, had to be developing high levels of equity leadership expertise at their school.

Derek asked his leadership team to privately rate themselves on the equity leadership expertise tool in table 4.2 from the point of view of their specific role. He also asked them to rate what they believed to be the average of the group they represented (teachers, administrators, or counselors).

The results indicated none of the team members felt they had the expertise necessary to make sound decisions about how to accelerate student success. Even the district administrator admitted she rated herself at a level two. The team noted that their assessment of their colleagues' expertise was also low. It was an open secret that the school and district did not have the expertise needed to move the needle for historically lower-achieving students.

The best antidote to the Christmas Tree Effect is defining the *thing of the thing* to be the development of *equity leadership knowledge and expertise* in the adults who serve those students.

**Table 4.3** Guidance for Developing Equity Leadership Expertise

| Plan Questions | Answer | Guidelines from the Research and Best Practice |
|---|---|---|
| What? | Equity leadership knowledge and expertise | For each role, provide deep, thoughtful professional learning on how to think about the challenge of getting to *X*. Provide a few high-impact, lower-prep strategies shared by everyone in that role for each layer of the acceleration formula. |
| Who? | TLC | Teachers, leaders, and counselors (TLC) in the first phase<br>(The *C* includes other wrap-around service providers.) |
| Where? | Job-embedded | On campuses, in classrooms, or in counseling centers<br>(People are more successful at implementing new skills if they learn them in a job-embedded way.) |
| When? | Five-plus year cycles | 1. Leaders preview content the year prior to expected implementation.<br>2. Next, staff attends a Summer Kickoff Institute.<br>3. Staff practices new summer skills and receives feedback during school year.<br>4. At the end of the school year, the leadership team reviews the previous year and plans refinements for next year. |
| How? | Accelerated improvement | Nonthreatening practice and frequent feedback throughout the year<br>• Ex. lesson study, guided planning, facilitated learning walks, data inquiry cycle, side by side coaching/mentoring<br>• Ten hours of *new* information per year (ideally during summer) with four hours of doing (guided planning, trying strategies with feedback, facilitated observations of colleagues in action, etc.) for every hour new information = 40 total hours per year each for T, L, and C.<br>• No less than five years to reach high levels of knowledge and expertise, assuming no change in direction or competing priorities |

## How to Develop Systemwide Equity Leadership Expertise

Based on the ideas that Derek and Alma explored together, table 4.3 outlines the design parameters the team followed to develop a plan to cultivate equity leadership expertise on campus.

## Did True HS Get to $X$?

The answer is yes! Here is how True HS got there.

The members of the school action team, minus the student (who graduated) and the parent (who moved), spent the entire next school year developing their equity leadership expertise. They read common books and articles, visited campuses with promising student results, and invited a couple of experts in the field to speak with them at a weekend retreat. They each also obtained a coach, a respected person in their own job responsibility, who had at least ten years of experience as an impactful equity leader in $T$, $L$, or $C$ (teaching, leading or counseling).

At the end of that year, they designed a professional learning plan that strictly adhered to the guidance shared in table 4.3. Their focus was vertical and horizontal alignment of learning and guidance expectations for students, as well as teaching and counseling expectations for the adults with the greatest impact on students. Each year, they added no more than one small twist to the focus of the previous year, if anything at all. Their goal was to create conditions for teachers, leaders, and the counseling team to become deeply immersed in a small set of highly impactful equity practices with a thorough understanding of why and how they are important to the school mission and to student life options.

In four years True HS's student demographics remained primarily African American and lower income; however, True HS went from having an average of 30 percent of their graduates meet university-eligibility criteria to graduating 60 percent university-eligible students. This was impressive to everyone but even more satisfying for Derek was the fact that African American students went from 15 to 50 percent, the state average for all students! Talk about getting to $X$! Even more meaningful is the fact that this trajectory continued for three more years under Derek's principalship and for several years after the transition to a new principal.

# Chapter 4

## Prologue

Eventually, most of the members of the leadership team moved on to become expert equity leaders in other schools, at the district, or in other districts. As for Derek and Alma, they eventually landed in the same district, both as assistant superintendents. Derek led Education Services, and Alma was at the office of Research and Evaluation.

They, along with the True HS team members, remained professional and personal friends. They all met at least once a year to reaffirm that the Christmas Tree Effect was a common systemic inequity trap, no matter what new position they accepted. Even after ten years of annual get-togethers and becoming the go-to people in their respective roles, none of the group members claimed to have reached the highest level of equity leadership expertise. However, they agreed on three major lessons from their experiences together:

- The best way to get to $X$ is to strategically select a very, very few efforts—ideally, one approach—and focus on quality implementation for a long time. Stay the course.
- Nothing good for students or adults comes from piling on initiatives.
- *The thing of the thing* must be to develop equity leadership knowledge and expertise so that leaders are equipped to make the wisest decisions about how to design a school system that propels historically lower-achieving students to get to $X$ *marks the spot.*

## Summary

This chapter explores the mysteries about why it seems that the more schools and districts try to help students get to $X$, the less student achievement improves. Derek Hart and his dear friend and thought partner, Alma, go on a quest to figure out why there existed a palatable culture of disengagement among adults and students at True HS. Could this explain their persistent student achievement gap? Their investigation led them to deeply study the effect of program overload on the attitudes and behaviors of adults and students. This chapter offers strategies for leaders to develop a brain trust of equity leadership knowledge and expertise in schools and districts so historically lower-achieving students benefit from the most sound and impactful decisions.

## Equity Concepts

- The Christmas Tree Effect—the impact that school systems have on staff and administrators when they expend human and financial resources on too many priorities, simultaneously or in rapid succession.

- Equity Leadership and Knowledge Expertise—Novices and experts experience, perceive, and analyze challenges differently. The underdevelopment of equity leadership expertise is a primary explanation for leadership decisions that overload staff and students and leaders with too many priorities to positively impact students.

## Actionable Tools

Now is the time for you to check for the Christmas Tree Effect in your own school or district. We invite you and a team to use the online templates to understand more deeply the implications of the Christmas Tree Effect in your school or district. Locate the fillable templates at https://orendaed.org/WhereEquityLives/.

CHAPTER 5

# Misaligned Leadership
*Equity Hook: Equity Leadership Columns*

Have you ever wondered

- what the number one most common systemic inequity trap is;
- why collaborating with other education leaders can either be one of the most exhilarating professional experiences or can feel like torture;
- if dealing with leaders who value other things over getting students to $X$ is just part of the job; or
- how one negative person on a leadership team can tear down years of advancements toward providing all students with a premium education?

This chapter describes the last of the set of five most common systemic inequity traps identified through our study of studies. The title, "Misaligned Leadership," and the equity hook, "Equity Leadership Columns," are meant to invoke an image of the design and construction of a substantial structure. Imagine something grand and beautiful, like . . . a school district, for example. We do not refer to the physical school district building. We refer to the notion of a strong alliance among adults with a deeply-held mission to serve students, especially those who have historically experienced much lower levels of academic success.

CHAPTER 5

We save this systemic inequity trap for last because the first four all land here—with the degree of unity among the adults who lead the efforts to get all students to *X*. Here we confidently share a bold finding that comes directly from our study of three hundred schools and districts over twenty-five years.

> *Above all else in a school system, the likelihood of historically lower-achieving students reaching the highest academic levels is directly tied to the degree of alignment among a highly knowledgeable and cohesive group of key leaders in the system.*

In this chapter we explain how strong individual leaders are necessary but not the answer for getting students to *X*. Or as we wrote in *Shattering Inequities* (2018), "A star does not a constellation make!" This final story describes how leadership misalignment impacts historically lower-achieving students in profound ways.

## Aurora Unified School District (AUSD)

AUSD was infamous for years of district strife, chaos, and corruption. Then, in what seemed like a remarkable turnaround, it became the district with the most accelerated achievement growth in the county. The student body comprised 30% African American, 40% Latino, 20% White, and 10% Native American students. Eighty percent of the students came from lower-income homes.

Every student group was achieving between twenty-five– and one hundred–scale score points below grade level, except for one. The higher-income, mostly White students achieved one hundred points above grade level. The three superintendents who came and went during those five years encouraged many innovations. Investments were made in many initiatives, including the following:

- house structure (small-school concept)
- a mentoring program
- dual-language strand

- one-to-one technology
- parent centers
- extended after-school programs
- mobile health clinics

A great deal of time and money was spent on these initiatives, yet the data demonstrated that students did not reap academic benefits. We will spare you the sordid details, but midway through 2019, Dr. Nez was hired to be the "next new superintendent." She grew up in a working-class neighborhood not far from the district office. So she felt a personal and professional commitment to improving the education for students in her new district home.

She had attended AUSD as one of the small numbers of Native American students. This was back when the district had a reputation for being steady and effective with every student group. She was one of the beneficiaries of that strong program. She'd experienced the life-altering power of a solid and rich education and felt a duty to give all her students the same opportunity. Without a shadow of a doubt, she knew that high achievement was possible for all the students in her care. Upon her arrival to the district, she reviewed student achievement data and was privately almost inconsolable that only about one in ten Native American students was on grade level. All other demographic groups were woefully underachieving as well. The new superintendent had to address achievement as her first priority.

## An Empty Cabinet

Dr. Nez convened her cabinet. One of the previous superintendents had created the cabinet structure to promote a sense of unity and transparency across the district. This inclusive team consisted of the top leaders in the district, including the assistant superintendents of business, educational services, human resources, support services, and data and evaluation; the teachers' association president; the classified staff association president; a parent representative; and a student. On occasion, board members dropped in.

CHAPTER 5

At her first scheduled cabinet meeting, Dr. Nez brought her deep angst about students' unacceptable achievement to the team. As it happened, the board president attended this meeting. This cabinet structure was formed two years prior to her hiring, so she felt like the team could openly and honestly examine this daunting challenge and find a solution. That was not the case. Instead, members retreated to their individual roles and became defensive. Here are highlights of the discussion:

- Teacher Representative (ten-year veteran of district): "Teachers are always blamed for low achievement. But how can we do our best when things keep changing! We care for our students and are doing the best we can. The district starts something and never finishes it before we start something else. We don't get supported as we try to do what the district expects. We never feel confident about anything we are doing. No one seems to care about the challenges we have serving this community. It is all very unsettling and makes teachers retreat to their classrooms and do what they believe is best for their students."
- Assistant Superintendent of Human Resources (three years in the district): "You are correct. In the span of five years, every school has experienced at least one principal turnover, and assistant principals have left us as well. Also, every school lost teachers during that time. We have a revolving door at every school. I cannot fill the positions fast enough, and substitutes are scarce. Every day, we disperse students from classrooms without a teacher to other classrooms in small groups just to have a place for them to spend the day."
- Assistant Superintendent of Support Services (two years in the district): "I encouraged the house structure when I got here, but it has not been supported by school principals. I feel strongly that this is the most direct way to get student acceleration. We need to create the feeling of small schools in our large schools. We need to address the social and emotional needs of our students by

establishing closer relationship with adults. Our counselors and guidance teams need to have a greater presence."
- Assistant Superintendent of Education Services (six months in the district): "In my time here, I have seen a need to provide teachers with high-quality instructional materials. In my previous district, we provided professional learning on the use of instructional materials every year."
- Teachers' Association President: "See? There it is. It is always our fault!"
- Board President (newly installed midterm due to unexpected opening): "Did the work on the use of instructional materials improve achievement?"
- Assistant Superintendent of Education Services: "Yes, after three years, every group improved a bit each year, though the gap between demographic groups remained constant. That was our next step."
- Assistant Superintendent of Business (twenty years in the district): "Just tell me what you want me to do, and I'll do it."
- Assistant Superintendent of Data and Evaluation (eighteen years in the district): "Ditto."

This was the gist of the meeting. The parent and the classified association president did not speak during the meeting, and the student looked like she wanted to share but never did. Dr. Nez ended the cabinet meeting with an empty feeling in the pit of her stomach. She had a large cabinet, yet it felt very empty.

## Fond Memories

She reflected on her previous district where she'd served as assistant superintendent of educational services for seven years. Those were the most fulfilling years of her career (except for her teaching years, of course). That district accomplished so many goals—most notably, reducing the outcome gaps between lower-achieving students and grade-level proficiency. She felt proud of everything they'd accomplished, including the following:

1. They institutionalized that the floor for every student in the district was graduating with Cs or better in the entire university-preparatory course sequence. This way students could have every option available to them upon high school graduation.
2. They set a five-year target for cutting in half outcome gaps between the achievement of lower-achieving student demographic groups and grade-level proficiency.
3. They invested heavily in the development of equity leadership expertise in all school and district leaders.
4. They implemented tiered support levels to accelerate learning on grade-level expectations for struggling students without ever labeling and sorting them. Their design even provided stronger students with the ability to accelerate their achievement.

You will recognize these four accomplishments as solutions to the four systemic inequity traps described in the first four chapters of this book. Dr. Nez could not help but smile as she remembered everything that her previous district leadership group had accomplished. It was invigorating, satisfying, motivating, and fun! Her teammates were a blast! And the outcomes for students were incredible.

The initiatives in her previous district were the correct ones, but they were not the key to student success. The key was the incredible team of leaders she enjoyed so much. Over the years of working together, they had become a close, fierce family of equity champions, relentless about their mission. Even though her previous district was larger than her new district home, her previous district group of movers and shakers had a cabinet half the size of her current cabinet. In her previous district, the team that made things happen consisted of the

- superintendent;

- assistant superintendent of educational services;
- assistant superintendent of student support services;
- coordinator of professional learning; and
- a teacher coach (from the district office).

These five leaders did not even have an official group title (though they jokingly called themselves the "Taco Team," because they felt so invigorated when they were together, that they made it a point to get tacos from the food truck outside of the district office together every Tuesday (Taco Tuesday!). Everyone in the district just knew that they were the student learning brain trust, not because of position power but because of their deep equity leadership knowledge and expertise and obvious commitment to student acceleration. Their ideas got traction because they frequently consulted with others outside of their group at various stages of planning.

The superintendent frequently communicated with the board of education to make sure they were in alignment as well. But this small team, almost as the district default, accepted the ultimate responsibility for creating the conditions for getting all students to $X$. Dr. Nez reminisced about how comfortable, enjoyable, and exhilarating the work was with that team, even though it was far from easy. It was a mental and emotional rush whenever they were together. They formally met once a week but checked in with one another almost every day and even checked in about their learning acceleration plan on Taco Tuesdays!

Dr. Nez reflected on her previous district experience and realized that the power behind that small team in her previous district was not that the district had amazing leaders. Many of them were, of course. *But the secret to the district success was that they had a steadfast equity leadership column.*

### *Equity Leadership Column*

An *equity leadership column* is a small subset of all the leaders in a district. It is not usually the full district leadership team or superintendent's cabinet. It is a handful of equity champions—a small team of leaders who believe in a true, right, and just education for every student—holding the

# Chapter 5

right jobs. Like the physical columns that have survived on earth over two thousand years, the equity leadership column Dr. Nez remembered was a strong, aligned, steady, unyielding pillar made up of individual parts, each a support to and dependent on the other. They were a solid equity leadership column. The equity leadership column was a small piece of the district leadership that had a powerful influence on the district direction about how to get students to *X*.

Let us break down the equity leadership column components. In education there are rarely any absolutes because of the complexities of educating students in school systems. However, we will boldly offer a few "absolute" truths that explain how equity leadership columns can make or break the future for students, depending on whether they are weak or strong.

### *Absolute Truth No. 1: Superintendent Stability*

The base of the column is the superintendent and the board. It is almost cliché to say that the board and superintendent should be aligned. After all, the most important job of a board is to hire the superintendent. Yet, as in the case of AUSD, boards and superintendents do not always align. In fact, sometimes the board of education members experience conflict among themselves. This tees up the first absolute truth:

- One hundred percent of school systems getting to X have *long-term, stable superintendents*, according to our study of studies. Conversely, *not one* of our case studies demonstrated significant and sustained strides in closing outcome gaps with *revolving* superintendents.

A nonnegotiable piece of an equity leadership column is the superintendent. The national trend works against this absolute need for stability at the helm of a school system, as well as at the base of an effective equity leadership column. Almost 60 percent of superintendents in the United States remain in a district for four years or less, not enough time to fortify the base of the column (School Superintendent Demographics and Statistics in the United States).

In Dr. Nez's previous district, the superintendent led the district for fifteen years. He was supported by the board the entire time, with a couple of political ripples here and there. Overall, though, the superintendent was able to conceptualize, implement, perfect, and grow sustainable roots for just the four parts of their equity plans described in chapters one through four.

*Absolute Truth No. 2: Board of Education Reinforcement*
Getting students to X *marks the spot* is only possible with a sturdy and wide superintendent–school board base. The board of education must share the priority to get to X with the superintendent. They *must* agree on the *achievement floor* and the *conditions necessary* for getting all students to grade level or above.

In this metaphor the board and superintendent are one, serving as the base of the column. In the best scenario, they are two sides of the base of that one column, providing reinforcement from elements that may try to topple the column over. However, the reality is that some superintendents interact with boards whose members are not all vocal champions of providing every student with the premium education.

Plainly stated, this situation provides a low ceiling on accelerated achievement for historically struggling students. Superintendents require their board's support for district learning-acceleration plans. Effective superintendents communicate with board members during initiative planning and throughout the implementation phase. Following this "rule of no surprises" with boards increases the odds that members will back student acceleration plans. Effective superintendents make it their mission to find ways to appeal to every board member so that they support whatever it takes to provide a true, right, and just education for every student.

> *The stronger the base, the stronger the column. And the stronger the column, the longer it will remain standing. So the closer the alignment between the board and superintendent, the more effective the district will be at getting to X, and the more students will benefit.*

CHAPTER 5

What that means is that more than support, board members of exceptional school systems for historically lower-achieving students provide *reinforcement* to the superintendent and district. We know that board members represent the community, and, therefore, people with various interests continuously solicit board members' support. The board must listen to input *and, at the same time,* commit to the work the superintendent and the board agreed upon. It is not an easy job, but they must help reinforce the district course in order to advance meaningful student acceleration.

*Absolute Truth No. 3: Small Equity Leadership Columns Are Best*
Getting to $X$ requires a small team of key leaders with deep expertise in equity concepts and program design. Every member of the small team must believe in and be able to bring to fruition the board-superintendent vision for getting students to $X$. And they must be in sync with one another.

It would be remarkable if every district leader were at the expert level of the equity knowledge continuum. Excellent educators come with a variety of backgrounds, and the likelihood of attracting or growing 100 percent equity experts is miniscule. Fortunately, the finding of our study of studies is that getting to $X$ does not require that perfect 100 percent.

Getting to $X$ requires a small team of the right leaders in the right positions. The team need not be scaled by the size of the district. A district of seven schools can have a three-person equity leadership column, while a district of thirty schools might have five leaders in their column.

These can be titled leaders, like assistant superintendents of this or that. Or they can be leaders by virtue of their expertise with the acceleration formula, effectiveness, and credibility, regardless of title. But to get students to $X$, that team needs to exist and be reinforced by others in key positions in the district whose areas of responsibility are required by the student acceleration plan.

*Absolute No. 4: Site Leadership Respect*
Principals, assistant principals, and other school site leaders must believe in and implement the district true, right, and just plan for students. In

fact, the primary function of the equity leadership column is to establish the conditions for schools to offer powerful teaching and the necessary wraparound supports so that all students can experience a premium education.

Out of respect to the value of their school responsibilities, principals and other site leaders are part of the district leadership but should *not* be standing members of the small equity leadership column.

Principals and other site leaders are indispensable to getting students to *X*. But they must be able to focus on successfully implementing the district equity work at their schools. This requires finesse, adaptation, resistance, focus, and relationship building. This deportment is only possible if site leaders are present at their schools. Too often, site leaders are off campus for a variety of activities, such as district meetings, conferences, committee work, ceremonies, or the like.

Our study of studies found that almost 100 percent of schools that were successful with historically lower-achieving students had principals and other site leaders who were on campus almost all the of time. Conversely, schools with chronically absent principals were almost never successful at getting their students to *X*.

Site leaders should regularly be consulted at the various stages of the student acceleration planning—through implementation and until the final evaluation of initiatives. However, leaders without daily school-oversight responsibilities are best suited to comprise the equity leadership columns.

### *Absolute No. 5: Equity Leadership Column Integrity*

Getting students to *X* requires the leadership fortitude to address misalignments at any unit of influence across the school or district. A district working to get their students to *X* depends on *every leader in a position of influence*, beyond those that comprise the equity leadership column; all other leaders must believe in and earnestly implement the district design for getting to *X*. In other words, the entire district leadership team must follow the plan. Board members must reinforce superintendents in making leadership changes with urgency when a weak part of the equity leadership column—or of district leadership at large—is identified.

CHAPTER 5

## RETURNING TO THE CABINET

Dr. Nez shared the contrasts between her previous district experience with the small equity leadership column and this new structure with her cabinet. Interestingly, the cabinet agreed that the current structure was unwieldy and not very effective. They understood why the previous superintendent formed the cabinet the way he did but did not mind reconsidering the design.

The one strong request of the cabinet members was that they be consulted when plans could impact the people they represent. They did not feel they would lose anything by relinquishing the detailed discussions of plans to get students to $X$ to a small team of movers and shakers. After a few months, the superintendent identified four equity leadership column members and backcast planning began. Here was their plan:

- Immediately, the superintendent had a study session for the board members to share their equity plan and to get their feedback and approval.
- That spring, the equity leadership column members frontloaded leaders for the upcoming equity plan launch. They provided a series of seven equity knowledge sessions focused on alignment for all site and district leaders.
- Right afterward the plan was kicked off; all teachers and guidance staff from across the district attended a paid summer institute on curriculum and guidance alignment.
- That fall was the official launch of phase one of their plan. The district "tried on" a curriculum and guidance alignment system that provided regular data on the impact of their student acceleration plan for struggling students. They also monitored higher-achieving students to ensure they were thriving.

*Elegantly* is the best word to describe how AUSD rolled out their acceleration plan. Everyone directly responsible for student success was involved from the inception. As a result of this work, student achievement increased so much that the district could hardly believe it, even after the first year of implementation!

- By the end of the fourth year, student achievement increased so much that it made the local papers.
- Graduation rates increased from 83 to 95 percent, the same for all demographic groups (African American, Latino, White, and Native American).
- Dropout rates decreased from 10 to 3 percent, the same for all demographic groups.
- The percentage of students who graduated as university eligible increased from 18 to 48 percent, higher than the state average.
- By the sixth year, the district earned one of only four College Board awards in the United States and Canada for districts with the greatest increase in "nontraditional" students taking and passing Advanced Placement courses.

### Smile Now, Cry Later

One of the real-life consequences of visible success is that leaders get recruited to help other districts. And that is exactly what happened. After six years, members of the equity leadership column, as well as other district leaders, took promotions in other districts. Whereas the district used to have very few applicants for district administrative openings, now they were flooded with candidates. The human resources department led the hiring process, and the district hired five new administrators in one year.

By design, the new hires believed in the district student acceleration plan and hit the ground running. This was true for all of them—except for one. One of the new hires took the position as coordinator of professional learning, replacing one of the members of the equity leadership column. At first, he seemed like an asset. Soon it was clear that his hiring was a mistake.

Immediately after his hiring, he made it a point to build relationships. He met with key district and community leaders, including board members; the head of the local chamber of commerce; some principals;

and some of the leaders of the teacher and classified employee associations. He was confident and experienced. Later those traits expressed themselves in overconfidence and arrogance.

Most importantly, he vocally opposed some of the basic tenets of the learning acceleration plan. For example, for the sake of expediency, he was in favor of purchasing intervention programs for struggling students rather than going through the trouble of capacity building to implement the district acceleration plan. He purchased intervention materials for the entire district, sent them out to the schools, and scheduled an optional fifty-minute publisher's overview for staff. He did all of this without consulting anyone. Needless to say, that plan accelerated nothing but frustration.

In another example, he yielded to pressure from some staff to reduce the number of progress-monitoring assessments. He approved going from five short checks prior to the year-end exam (about every twenty-five teaching days) to three assessments set to occur at the start of the school year, at the end of the first semester, and then at the end-of-the-year exam. Talk about $1°\Delta$! These compromises were many more than one degree different from the intended design.

## One Misaligned Piece of the Column

In only one school year, the integrity of the learning acceleration plan was compromised. The members of the equity leadership column saw that the coordinator was not happy with them. So, as a member of the equity leadership column, Dr. Nez reminded him that he was part of a team of educators entrusted with leading their initiative to get all students to X. She explained that his actions were working against the goals of the district and creating instability in the equity leadership column, as well as the district. But it was clear that the coordinator felt he knew more than others, so he continued to make executive decisions independently, which put stress on the column and the district.

Dr. Nez tried to bring him into the fold through his first and second year with the district. Several highly effective administrators left the district because they could not work with that coordinator or because they would not follow his poor direction any longer. Equity leaders throughout the district were frustrated that the superintendent did nothing about him.

This resulted in hints of a lack of confidence in Dr. Nez's leadership, even among a few board members. But by that time, the coordinator had cultivated strong relationships with people with reputations for opposing anything the district promoted. Some of those relationships were with some heavy-politicking influencers. This made him dangerous to all employees, even the superintendent.

## A Broken Column

By the end of the that year, the overall district culture regressed almost to where it had been before Dr. Nez arrived. The integrity of the equity leadership column was compromised, negatively influencing one board member at the base of the column and two principals.

But the column completely toppled over when student achievement results were released. The district saw a decline in almost every achievement indicator. Their winning streak was broken in just two years. Students were hurt because of the coordinator's "small changes" to appease certain individuals and to elevate the coordinator's personal status.

This was Dr. Nez's "Not on my watch!" moment. She told a confidant, "You can mess with me. But I cannot stand for anyone hurting our students." We will spare you the details, but this coordinator stayed two additional years while Dr. Nez took the appropriate legal and political steps. Then he moved on.

## Did They Rebuild Their Column?

We would love to share that the district quickly recovered after that one leader departed. Unfortunately, that was not the case. As many as five years after this episode, AUSD continued to struggle to bring their equity leadership column "back to code." But regaining lost momentum is no small feat. As of the writing of this book, improvements at AUSD are slow but going in the correct direction.

After three more years, Dr. Nez moved to another district. She was soon joined by several members of her equity leadership column. After four years in this new district, they were able to replicate the successes they experienced at AUSD. This brought much-needed excitement to her new district community. This time, Dr. Nez placed the highest importance on frequently checking for fissures in the equity leadership column. She learned to immediately address anything or anyone who compromised the integrity of the column. In her new district, everyone knew that Dr. Nez would not accept misaligned leadership in or out of the column, which would get in the way of the district quest to provide all students with the premium education they so deserve.

## Where Are They Now?

Dr. Nez is going on her sixth year as superintendent in her district, and she has no plans to leave any time soon. Her equity leadership column continues to become fortified by the pride that comes from improving life options for historically lower-achieving students. As for that coordinator, what happened to him? He is now superintendent of a district several counties away. He calls Dr. Nez for advice about once a week. Each time he phones, she remembers the equity hook from *Shattering Inequities*, "Do you want to be right, or do you want to do right?" (Avelar La Salle and Johnson 2018). Then, she answers the phone and graciously helps him every time.

## Summary

This chapter describes the most common of the systemic inequity traps we identified through our study of studies—misaligned leadership. One hundred percent of every case study of successful districts getting students to $X$ had a small group of mover-and-shaker equity leaders who set the direction for the learning acceleration plan. In addition, every successful district had the reinforcement of their board, as well as key leaders from the district office to schools. Conversely, every case study of unsuccessful school systems had misaligned leadership. This chapter shares a true story of one superintendent who experienced a series of lessons about the implications that the architecture of an equity leadership column has on students getting to $X$. These lessons empowered her with the fortitude to address difficult staffing challenges with much more urgency than she had before.

## Equity Concept

- Equity Leadership Column—a small number of key members of district leadership with equity expertise who have the position or the influence to design and guide a school system's initiative to ensure that every student experiences the premium education that, historically, only some have received.

## Actionable Tools

Now is time for you to check for misaligned leadership in your own school or district. We invite you to gather a team together to use the online templates to think more deeply about the implications of the fifth and most significant of all the systemic inequity traps in your school or district. Locate the fillable templates at https://orendaed.org/WhereEquityLives/.

# Conclusion

In the pages of this book, we lay out achievable paths of possibilities and opportunities for equity leaders to create conditions that get all students to *X*—that magnificent place where educational equity lives. This will be when student demographics no longer predict achievement.

As equity leaders, you now have a rich treasure chest of knowledge about how to accelerate achievement for historically struggling students. You have the know-how to identify and shatter the five most common systemic inequity traps impeding the achievement of African American, Latino, Indigenous, and low-income students. As a result of your leadership, these students will be prepared for life options that are regularly only available to their more advantaged peers. You understand the power of the three simple questions:

1. What is the floor?
2. Under what conditions?
3. How aligned are YOU?

Wait! There is another question that we need to consider:

4. What is at the root of all systemic inequity traps?

The educational barriers to accelerating achievement for historically marginalized students land on one inescapable truth that lies deep below the waterline of any school system: educational policies and practices that advantage some student groups and disadvantage others are the result of a legacy of societal assumptions about people.

- Many educators believe that all students are equally capable of reaching high levels of achievement. But not all do.
- Many educators expect all students to excel in school and will do what it takes to make that so. But not all do.
- Many education leaders see themselves as the people whose urgent charge it is to change the odds for historically undereducated kids. But we know that not all do.

A hard fact is that at the core of every systemic inequity trap are adult beliefs, expectations, and perceptions that result in systemic practices that impact students. Why, then, is this not a book about how to change minds and hearts? Why spend so many pages on understanding the systemic inequity traps that are fundamentally the result of adult decisions based on beliefs, expectations, and perceptions?

Here is why. We live in the real world of schools and districts. We understand that educators are mere mortals, complex and imperfect, as we all are. Whether we are aware of it or not, we "other" people—we all harbor thoughts and feelings about different people based on upbringing, outside inputs, or our personal experience. And the more our identity is tied to those assumptions, the more resistant our brain is to revising them. In fact, the more people challenge our core beliefs, the more committed we become to those beliefs. That is simply how the brain works.

## Changing Minds and Hearts

How, then, do we change the minds and hearts of people who make decisions based on the belief that some people inherently have a greater capacity for intellectual pursuits than others? It is simple. We cannot. No one can change another person's mind about anything. Fortunately, we do not have to.

Here is how equity leaders can make a difference:

1. Change conditions—make sure that every student receives a premium educational experience.

2. Outcomes change—engage in open conversations with colleagues who express skepticism, disbelief, or surprise when students surpass expectations. Help them process their questions.

3. Minds and hearts change—each time students exceed expectations, people naturally reflect on their assumptions. In time most educators will revise their limiting biases and "exceptions" will become the new normal.

Our school systems are improving, just at a pace where not all current students will benefit. Let us all commit to engaging in these three steps over and over again to apply authentic and positive pressure to accelerate that rate of improvement and student achievement. We hope that you connected with the true cases in the chapters of this book. And we wish with *all our might* that, through your courageous leadership, the insights and practical strategies shared through each story translate into a world where demographics, once and for all, no longer determine destiny.

*May all our students soon reach X, the magnificent spot where equity lives.*

# Appendix A

## Study of Studies Methodology

The key to shattering educational inequities is the ability to identify systemic traps that halt the ability of some students to access a premium education that is an entitlement for other students. The content of this book is based on over three hundred school and district studies conducted over twenty-five years. We (the authors) and the skilled team of educational specialists at Orenda Education (formerly Principal's Exchange) conducted studies to answer the following three questions:

- *What are the patterns of student success (or lack of success)?* First, we reviewed student outcomes over time to understand the student experience and to identify the demographic patterns in the data, if they exist. (As a point of fact, *every* school and district in the over three hundred studies reviewed for this book exhibited patterns in student outcomes by demographic group.)
- *What systems best explain those patterns?* Next, we collected data and various types of information to identify the *structural inequities* that exist as part of the way a school or district operates. Sometimes these traps have been obvious, such as in the tale of two boys told in the preface. Other times, systemic inequity traps are much more difficult to identify but have a more profound and long-term impact on changing systems and changing lives.
- *What recommendations from research and best practice can increase student success?*

# Appendix A

## *Data Collection*

To respond to the first question, *student success profiles* are defined very broadly and depend on whether the schools are elementary or secondary. Profiles are understood through a collection of a wide variety of quantitative data points, including standardized measures of achievement, grades, course-taking patterns, transcript analyses, discipline records, on-track reports for graduation and university-eligibility, and many standard data sets.

Concurrently, we round out our profiling of student success by group, gathering qualitative data through interviews and focus groups of staff and students. Parents take online surveys when that is possible. We shadow a stratified random sampling of students through their school day, in and out of classrooms, and make general campus observations at different times on different days.

We approach each of the other two main guiding questions in like fashion, with a variety of traditional data and "other data" (Johnson and Avelar La Salle 2010). Other data refers to traditional data used in unconventional ways, data from sources not often accessed (such as qualitative information), or combination data. The questions are not linear. They interrelate, and, as the case story is revealed, the answers to each question inform the others.

## *Seesaw Inquiry Process*

What does that process of getting the answers to the guiding questions look like in practice? We implement what we call "seesaw inquiry" (Avelar La Salle and Johnson 2018). Using this process, we peel back layers of systems' "wallpaper" (Johnson and Avelar La Salle 2010) to see if we find cracks in the system that could explain student outcome gaps. Figure A.1 depicts that process.

First, we ask a basic question, such as, "Do student outcome differences exist here?" Then we collect quantitative and qualitative data that inform that question. This then leads to a deeper question and more complex data collection, etcetera. Hunches are derived from each data dive until time or data run out. Finally, all the data related to the hunches are triangulated to see which hunches can be confirmed multiple ways,

Appendix A

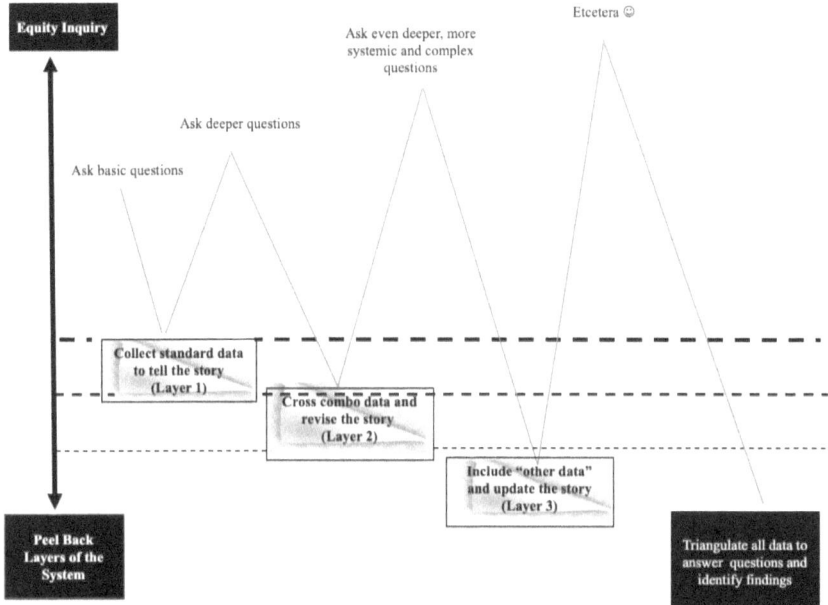

Figure A.1. Seesaw Inquiry Process

using all the data gathered. Only then are hunches elevated to the level of answers or findings, corresponding to our guiding questions.

## A Study of Studies

We now have over three hundred multiple-methods case studies, which are rich with information gathered from schools and districts representing almost every conceivable context. For this book we mined each of those studies for answers to the second case study question, "What systems best explain the student profiles here?" We conducted a thematic analysis to identify the common findings. Here is a general overview of the comprehensive case study review process:

1. Each case study was coded on a variety of contextual variables, such as size, geography, and demographics, to check for patterns among the findings by variable.

## Appendix A

2. We then reread each study and pulled out the findings regarding systemic obstacles (inequity traps) to a premium education for all students.

3. Findings were clustered into thematic groupings and coded by theme.

4. We listed the number of instances of each group of systemic obstacles from high to low. The first five (the material for this book) were observed in over 90% of the studies. The next most frequent themes ranged from only 10% to 40% and are not included in this book.

5. Finally, the contextual variables were crossed with the themes to look for patterns. No patterns were found, meaning that the groups of systemic barriers applied equally in all contexts.

This book is based on the findings of the study of studies just described. It provides a rich and textured description of each of the top five systemic inequity traps in school systems that limit life options for historically lower-achieving students.

# References

Agustin, M. Z., and M. A. Agustin. 2009. "Algebra and Precalculus Skills and Performance in First-Semester Calculus." *International Journal of Case Method and Application* XXI (3): 222–36.

Avelar La Salle, R., and R. S. Johnson. 2018. *Shattering Inequities: Real-World Wisdom for School and District Leaders.* Lanham: Rowman and Littlefield.

Bengston, D. H., L. M. Westphal, and M. J. Dockry. 2020. "Back from the Future: The *Backcasting* Wheel for Mapping a Pathway to a Preferred Future." *World Futures Review* 12 (3): 270–78.

Blankstein, A. M., Noguera, P., & Kelly, L. (2016). *Excellence through equity: Five principles of courageous leadership to guide achievement for every student.* Ascd.

Byrk, A. S. 1993. *A View from the Elementary Schools: The State of Reform in Chicago. A Report of the Steering Committee, Consortium on Chicago School Research.* Consortium on Chicago School Research.

California State Department of Education. 2022. "COVID Relief Funding Summary Sheet." Federal Stimulus Funding (website). Last modified June 15, 2022. https://www.cde.ca.gov/fg/cr/relieffunds.asp.

Carnevale, A. P., J. Strohl, A. Gulish, M. Van Der Werf, and K. P. Campbell. 2019. *The Unequal Race for Good Jobs.* Georgetown University Center on Education and the Workforce. https://cew.georgetown.edu/wp-content/uploads/ES-The_Unequal_Race_for_Good_Jobs.pdf.

Coleman, J., E. Q. Campbell, C. J. Hobson, J. McPartland, A. M. Mood, F. D. Weinfeld, and R. L. York. 1966. *Quality of Educational Opportunity.* Washington, DC: US Department of Health, Education and Welfare.

Dorn, E., B. Hancock, J. Sarakatsannis, and E. Viruleg. 2020. "COVID-19 and Student Learning in the United States: The Hurt Could Last a Lifetime." McKinsey & Company (website). https://www.mckinsey.com/industries/education/our-insights/covid-19-and-student-learning-in-the-united-states-the-hurt-could-last-a-lifetime.

Edmonds, R. (2020). Characteristics of effective schools. In *The school achievement of minority children* (pp. 93–104). Routledge.

Elmore, R. F. 1996. "Getting to Scale with Good Educational Practice." *Harvard Educational Review* 66 (1): 1–26.

# References

Fletcher, J. M., and G. Lyon. 1998. "Reading: A Research-Based Approach." In *What's Gone Wrong with America's Classrooms*, edited by W. M. Evers, 49–90. Stanford: Hoover Institution Press.

FRAM. 2022. "FRAM History." FRAM Trusted since 1934. Accessed April 2022. https://www.fram.com/about-us/history/.

Gilchrist, Cowan, and Naveh-Benjamin. 2008. "Working Memory Capacity for Spoken Sentences Decreases with Adult Aging: Recall of Fewer, but not Smaller Chunks in Older Adults." *Memory* 16: 773–87.

Goldberg, D., and D. Brewer. 1999. "Teacher Licensing and Student Achievement." In *Better Teachers, Better Schools*, edited by M. Kanstroroom and C. E. Finn Jr., 83–102. Washington, DC: Fordham Foundation.

Hartl, S., and C. Riley. 2021. "High-Quality Curriculum Is a Transformation Tool for Equity." ASCD. https://www.ascd.org/el/articles/high-quality-curriculum-is-a-transformation-tool-for-equity.

Hatti, J. 2003. "Teachers Make a Difference: What Is the Research Evidence?" Paper presented at Building Teacher Quality: What Does the Research Tell Us ACER Research Conference, Melbourne.

Hodges, T. 2018. "School Engagement Is More than Just Talk." Gallup. https://www.gallup.com/education/244022/school-engagement-talk.aspx.

Johnson, R. S., and R. Avelar La Salle. 2010. *Data Strategies to Uncover and Eliminate Hidden Inequities: The Wallpaper Effect*. Thousand Oaks: Corwin.

Juel, C. 1988. "Learning to Read and Write: A Longitudinal Study of 54 Children from First through Fourth Grades." *Journal of Educational Psychology* 80 (4): 437–47.

Konstantopoulos, S. 2005. *Trends of School Effects on Student Achievement: Evidence From Nls:72, Hsb:82, and Hels:92*. Boston: Boston College, IZA Department of Labor.

Lezotte, L. (1991). *Correlates of effective schools*. The First and second generation effective schools products, Ltd., Okemos, MI.

Marzano, R., T. Waters, and B. McNulty. 2005. *School Leadership That Works: From Research to Results*. Alexandria, VA: Association of Supervision and Curriculum Development.

Miller, G. A. 1956. "The Magical Number Seven, Plus or Minus Two: Some Limits on Our Capacity for Processing Information." *Psychological Review* 63: 81–97.

Mulhern, C. 2020. *Beyond Teachers: Estimating Individual Guidance Counselors' Effects on Educational Attainment*. Boston: Harvard University.

National Institutes of Health. n.d. "Office of Management, Human Resources." Leadership and Management Suggested Competency Models. Accessed August 2022. https://hr.nih.gov/working-nih/competencies/occupation-specific/suggested-competency-models.

Peters, R. L. 2002. "News +." Robert L. Peters (website). Accessed April 2022. http://robertlpeters.com/news/?s=design+culture+future&x=0&y=0.

Salvatore, S. C., W. E. Martin, V. L. Ruiz, P. Sullivan, and H. Sitkoff. 2020. *Racial Segregation in Public Education in the United States*. United States Government, US Department of the Interior, National Park Service. Washington, DC: National Register, History and Education.

# References

Santayana, G. 1905. *The Life of Reason*. Vol. 2. New York: Scribner's Sons.

Schunn, C. D., and M. M. Patchan. 2009. "Expert-Novice Studies: An Educational Perspective." In *Psychology of Classroom Learning: An Encyclopedia*. Detroit, MI: Macmillan Reference.

Siegler, R. S., and M. Chen. 2012. "Early Predictors of High School Mathematics Achievement. *Association of Psychological Science* 23 (7).

Webb, N. L. 2002. "Depth-of-Knowledge Levels for Four Content Areas." *Language Arts* 28 (March).

Zippia Careers. 2022. "Assistant Principal Demographics and Statistics in the U.S." Zippia The Career Expert. https://www.zippia.com/assistant-principal-jobs/demographics/.

# Index

*Page locators in italics indicate figures and tables*

acceleration approaches, 66, 66–67, 68, 98; eight opportunities, 70; and equity leadership columns, 103–5; student-acceleration-plan goals, 32
acceleration formula, 67–71, 69
achievement/outcome gaps, 1–3, 7–8, 78; and data systems, 9, 11–12, 30; and intervention-type curriculum, 55, 67; and misaligned leadership, 100; and planning approaches, 34, 40, 43–44; and tracking, 58, 66
actionable tools, 7, 32, 48, 72, 91, 109
alignment, 6, 31, 82, 94, 99–100, 111; for site and district leaders, 104; vertical and horizontal, 89. *See also* misaligned leadership
apathy, culture of, 74, 77–80, 84
Are You Lined Up? concept, 6–7
assessment, 2, 68; and data systems, 9–10, 18–19, 21, 23, 28–29, 31; frequency of, 19, 23, 28–29, 106; new tracking vs. acceleration, 68; progress-monitoring practices, 9, 15–18, 16–17
assistant principals, 37–38
attendance zones, 50–51

baby step planning, 4, 33–34, 36, 40
Backcast, Don't Forecast equity hook, 32
backcasting, 37–40, 44, 48, 104
baseline achievement level, 37, 48
beliefs and expectations, 2, 5, 34, 283; at core of systemic inequity, 57–58, 83, 111–12; floor, 11–12; institutional, 33–34, 36; oversimplified, 75–76; and rituals, 14
benchmarks, commercial, 28
best practices, 2, 24, 76, 88, 115
board of education, 96, 101–2, 103, 104
Bryk, Anthony S., 76

cabinet structure, 95–97, 104–5

# Index

CARES Act, *42*, 47
Christmas tree effect, 4, 6, 73–91; activity does not equal accomplishment, 74–76; discussion protocol, 81–83; multiple initiatives, 6, 76, 79, 84–87, *85*, 90, 94–85; novice-expert continuum, 84–87, *85*, *86*; program shopping, 6, 84, 87; and too many supports, 79–81
"Christmas Tree Schools" (Bryk), 76
chunks of information, 80
chunks of school year, 18, 39–40, 45
cognitive threat, 21, *29*, *88*
collaboration, 18, *23–24*, 31, 93, 98; lack of, 95–97
compliance, 9, 31, 33, 38, 41, 81
continuous-improvement practices, 9
COVID pandemic, 22; and funding, 40–41, *42–43*, 44; and harmful tracking, 58, 59–60
curriculum: intervention, 41, 43; remedial, 67; and tracking, 55, *61*, 67, 70

data practices, 5, 116; collaboration around, 18; data rituals, 15, 18–22, *23–25*, 31; integrity of, 20–21, 27, 32; logical data collection, 15–18, *16–17*; nested data systems, 19–22, *20*, 31, *85*. See also symbolic data systems
data reflection sessions (DRS), 19, *24*, *25*, *28*, *85*
deficit areas, addressing, 67
demographics, shifting, 50–52
differentiation, 53–56; advanced option, 53–56, *61–63*, 64; EL/Intervention A and B, 54, 55; grade-level option, 54–55, *61*; special house, 54, 55
district leadership, 102–3
district office staff, *23–25*; and nested data systems, *20*, 21–22
diversity, views on, 52
"dumbing down," concerns about, 51, 52, 54

Elementary and Secondary School Emergency Relief Fund (ESSER), 41–45, *42–43*, 47
Emperor's New Clothes equity hook, 4, 9, 10, 31
employee associations, 26
equity, defined, 8. *See also* floor; premium education; "*X* marks the spot" goal/getting to *X*
equity champions/leaders, 3–7, 46, 59, 73–74, 83; five data questions for, 15–17, *16–17*; and law of straight lines, *66*, 66–67; threshold of expertise required of, 84; vigilance required of, 5, 72. *See also* leadership

128

equity hooks: Backcast, Don't Forecast, 32; Emperor's New Clothes, 4, 9, 10, 31; A Rose by Any Other Name, 49, 50, 58; The Thing of the Thing, 73, 82–83, 86–87, 90. *See also* equity leadership columns

equity knowledge level, 51, 57, 64, 65, 84, 102, 104

equity leadership columns, 93, 99–109; and acceleration approaches, 103–5; board of education reinforcement, 101–2; components, 100–105; integrity of, 103; and misaligned leadership, 106–7; rebuilding after misalignment, 107–8; site leadership respect, 102–3; small size as best, 102; superintendent stability, 100–101. *See also* misaligned leadership

equity leadership expertise, *86*, 87–90, *88*, 98–99

equity vision, 33–34, 56

expertise: and data, 15; equity leadership, *86*, 87–90, *88*, 98–99; lack of, and tracking, 57–58; novice-expert continuum, 84–87, *85*, *86*; threshold of required, 84

feedback, 15, *29*, *68*

five-year plans, 37, *88*, 98

floor, *4, 5*, 11–13, *13*, 31, 111; clarity of, *28*; and equity leadership column, 101; institutionalization of, 98; for students with learning differences, 35, 39–40. *See also* premium education; "$X$ marks the spot" goal/getting to $X$

forecasting, 37–38, 40; and funding, 41–45; and legal requirements, 31, 40, 45–46

funding, 40–45, *42–43*, *45*

Gallup poll of teachers (2018), 79–80

gap-filling tutoring, 67, *68*

Governor's Emergency Education Relief Fund (GEER), *42, 43, 47*

guest teachers, *24*

historically lower-achieving students, 1–6; characteristics of impactful schools, 1–2, *2*; and data systems, 9–12, *16–17*, 18–19, 22, *23–25*, 27, 30–31; and misaligned leadership, 93–94, 101–3; and planning, 5, 34, 40, 47–48; and tracking, 49–50, 57–60, 72, 85

house structure, 54, 55, 94, 96–97

immigrants, 1850s, 57

individualized educational or 504 plans, 54

inequity traps, *4*; beliefs and expectations at core of, 57–58, 83, 111–12; "modern" versions of, 3, 56–57, 72; systemic, 1–10, 31, 47–50, 58, 65, 73, *86*, 89, 93–94, 98, 108–12, 115. See also *specific inequity traps*
institutional beliefs, 33–34, 36
integrity: of data practices, 20–21, 27, 32; of equity leadership columns, 103; and misaligned leadership, 106–7
intelligence quotient (IQ), 57

job-embedded skills, *88*

leadership, *2*; absences, 75, 103; district, 102–3; equity leadership expertise, *86*, 87–90, *88*, 98–99; feeling of being ill-prepared, 49, 51–52; site leaders, 20, *20*, 20–22, 102–3; *T, L,* or *C* (teaching, leading or counseling), *88*, 89. See also equity champions/leaders; equity leadership columns; misaligned leadership
learning differences, 34–35, 54, 57
linguistic and visual metaphors, 4

mandates, 10, 40, 41, 45; unsound, 59–60
materials, *68*, *85*, 97, 106
minds and hearts, changing, 112–13

misaligned leadership, *4*, 93–109; compromised integrity, 106–7; and multiple initiatives, 94–95; rebuilding equity leadership column, 107–8; "*X* marks the spot" goal/getting to *X*, 93, 94, 99–104, 108. See also equity leadership columns; leadership

nested data systems, 19–22, *20*, 31, *85*; anticipated challenges and systemic solutions for, *23–25*
new tracking. See tracking, new
novice-expert continuum, 84–87, *85*, *86*

one degree delta (10Δ), 27–29, *29*, 31, 58, 106
Orenda Education, 3, 115

placement considerations, 17, 22, 53–55, *61–62*
planning, *4*, 5, 33–48; baby-step approach, *4*, 33–34, 36, 40; for baseline achievement level, 37; and funding, 40–45, *42–43*, *45*; intermediate and end goals, 44–45; "realistic and attainable" goals, 38, 40
potential, as term, 12, 35
predictors of success, 17, *17*, 22
premium education, 7–8, 113, 115, 118; characteristics of high-impact schools, 2, *2*; and

Christmas tree effect, 76, 79, 81–82; and data systems, 12, 22, 30; and misaligned leadership, 93, 101, 103, 108; and planning, 44; and tracking, 56, 65; vision and mission statements, 12, 26. *See also* floor; "*X* marks the spot" goal/getting to *X*
pretending, 10
principals, 37–38
program shopping, 6, 84, 87. *See also* Christmas tree effect
progress-monitoring practices, 9, 15–18, *16–17*

"realistic and attainable" goals, 38, 40
"research-based" programs, 7
reverse-mainstreaming, 34–35
rituals for data collection, 14–15, 18–22, *23–25*, 31
A Rose by Any Other Name equity hook, 49, 50, 58
"rule of no surprises," 101

Santayana, George, 57
school districts, structure of, 93
seesaw inquiry process, 116–17, *117*
segregated schools, 57
*Shattering Inequities: Real World Wisdom for School and District Leaders* (Avelar La Salle and Johnson), 3, 12, 22, 59, 108

site leadership, 20, *20,* 20–22, 102–3
speech and language needs, 34–35
straight lines, law of, *66,* 66–67, 70
structural inequities, 115. *See also* inequity traps
student-acceleration-plan goals, 32
student perceptions, *63*
study of studies, 3, 7, 33, 48, 57, 94, 115–18, 117–18
success, *62*; patterns of, 115; predictors of, 17, *17,* 22
summer programs, 45, *47*
superintendents, 56–57; stability required, 100–101
supports, *2*; board of education as, 101–2; and Christmas tree effect, 79–81; and data practices, 11, 12, 14, 19, 22; tiered, *69,* 69–70, 98
symbolic data systems, *4, 5,* 9–32; Emperor's New Clothes equity hook, 4, 9, 10, 31; and floor, 11–12; and historically lower-achieving students, 9–12, *16–17,* 18–19, 22, *23–25,* 27, 30–31; and one degree delta (10Δ) changes, 27–29, *29,* 31; and rituals, 14–15; for show rather than impact, 10; and supports, 11, 12, 14, 19, 22. *See also* data practices

*T, L,* or *C* (teaching, leading or counseling), *88,* 89
teacher assignments, 55–56
teacher teams, *20,* 21
The Thing of the Thing equity hook, 73, 82–83, 86–87, 90
tiered support, *69,* 69–70, 98
Title I Blue Ribbon Award, 70
tracking: and curriculum, 55, *61,* 67, 70; historical, 49–50, 57–60, 72, *85*; and unsound mandates, 59–60
tracking, new, 4, 6, 49–53; "curvy line" approach, *66,* 66–67; vs. differentiation, 53–56; litmus test for, 60–65, *61–63*; new tracking vs. acceleration, *68*; placement considerations, 17, 22, 53–55, *61–62*; work habits criterion, 55, *62,* 64
"true, right, and just education," 5, 7, 8, 43; equity leadership column, 99–102; and tracking, 66–72, 76

Under What Conditions? concept, 5–6

vision and mission statements, 12, 26

What's the Floor? concept, *4,* 5, 11–13
work habits criterion, 55, *62,* 64

"*X* marks the spot" goal/getting to *X,* 19, 26, 30, 33; and Christmas tree effect, 76, 81, 84, 90; expertise required, 84; and misaligned leadership, 93, 94, 99–104, 108; and planning, 33, 41, 43–44, *44, 47,* 48. *See also* floor; premium education

# About the Authors

**Robin Avelar La Salle** earned her PhD in education from Stanford University and is the founder and president of a technical assistance organization with a twenty-five-year history of partnering with schools and districts that serve historically lower-achieving students. Her career as an equity warrior is captured in her 2018 book, *Shattering Inequities: Real-World Wisdom for School and District Leaders*, written with Ruth S. Johnson.

**Ruth Johnson** is a nationally known expert in the use of data to promote equity. She is the author of several books, including *Data Strategies to Uncover and Eliminate Hidden Inequities: The Wallpaper Effect* (with coauthor Dr. Avelar La Salle) and *Using Data to Close the Achievement Gap*, a bestselling book.

www.ingramcontent.com/pod-product-compliance
Lightning Source LLC
Chambersburg PA
CBHW032028230426
43671CB00005B/232